SpringerBriefs in Anthropology

SpringerBriefs in Anthropology and Ethics

More information about this series at http://www.springer.com/series/11496

To My friend
Nadine !
:)

Susan Dewey • Tiantian Zheng
Treena Orchard

Sex Workers and Criminalization in North America and China

Ethical and Legal Issues in Exclusionary Regimes

Susan Dewey
University of Wyoming
Laramie, Wyoming, USA

Tiantian Zheng
Sociology/Anthropology Department
State University of New York
Cortland, USA

Treena Orchard
School of Health Studies
Western University
London, ON, Canada

ISSN 2195-0806 ISSN 2195-0814 (electronic)
SpringerBriefs in Anthropology
ISBN 978-3-319-25761-7 ISBN 978-3-319-25763-1 (eBook)
DOI 10.1007/978-3-319-25763-1

Library of Congress Control Number: 2015956638

Springer Cham Heidelberg New York Dordrecht London
© The Author(s) 2016
This work is subject to copyright. All rights are reserved by the Publisher, whether the whole or part of the material is concerned, specifically the rights of translation, reprinting, reuse of illustrations, recitation, broadcasting, reproduction on microfilms or in any other physical way, and transmission or information storage and retrieval, electronic adaptation, computer software, or by similar or dissimilar methodology now known or hereafter developed.
The use of general descriptive names, registered names, trademarks, service marks, etc. in this publication does not imply, even in the absence of a specific statement, that such names are exempt from the relevant protective laws and regulations and therefore free for general use.
The publisher, the authors and the editors are safe to assume that the advice and information in this book are believed to be true and accurate at the date of publication. Neither the publisher nor the authors or the editors give a warranty, express or implied, with respect to the material contained herein or for any errors or omissions that may have been made.

Printed on acid-free paper

Springer International Publishing AG Switzerland is part of Springer Science+Business Media (www.springer.com)

Abstract

Sex work continues to provoke controversial legal and public policy debates worldwide that raise fundamental questions about the state's role in protecting individual rights, status quo social relations, and public health. This book unites ethnographic research from China, Canada, and the United States to argue that criminalization results in a totalizing set of negative consequences for sex workers' health, safety, and human rights. Such consequences are enabled through the operations of an exclusionary regime, a dense coalescence of punitive forces that involves both governance, in the form of the criminal justice system and other state agents, and dynamic interpersonal encounters in which individuals both enforce and negotiate stigma-related discrimination against sex workers. Chapter 2 demonstrates how criminalization harms sex workers by isolating their work to potentially dangerous locations, fostering mistrust of authority figures, further limiting their abilities to find legal work and housing, and restricting possibilities for collective rights-based organizing. Criminalized sex workers report police harassment, seizure of condoms, and adversarial police-sex worker relations that enable others to abuse them with impunity. Chapter 3 describes how sex workers negotiate these restrictions on their rights and personal autonomy via their arrest avoidance and client management strategies, self-treatment of health issues, selective mutual aid, rights-based organizing, and entrenchment in sex work or other criminalized activities. Chapter 4 describes how researchers working in countries or locales that criminalize sex work face ethical concerns as well as barriers to their work at the practical, institutional, and political levels.

Acknowledgments

We have spent most of our careers working with women involved in sex work and in the process have benefitted enormously from the generosity and collective wisdom shared with us by hundreds of sex workers, research colleagues, activists, healthcare and social services providers, and criminal justice professionals who work directly with the women. We hope that this book is itself a respectful acknowledgment of the time and energy others have shared with us. First and foremost, we all remain grateful for, and inspired by, the courage and candor of the women we have worked with over the years. We will be forever in their debt and hope that findings presented here constitute a small step toward doing justice to the complexities of their everyday lived experiences as they navigate criminal justice, healthcare, and social services systems that stigmatize, punish, or exclude them at every turn.

Susan and Treena would like to thank the University of Wyoming's Office of Research & Economic Development for a grant that allowed them to spend essential time together in London, Ontario, discussing this project, and provided small honoraria to women we interviewed as part of this project. This book would not have been possible without receipt of these funds. Susan is extremely grateful to her colleagues and teachers—at the University of Wyoming, on East Colfax Avenue, and in myriad Denver city offices—who unfailingly provide with her the inspiration and support needed to do this work. Susan's students are some of her greatest teachers, and while it is impossible to thank them all here, this project benefitted tremendously from assistance in the form of transcription, coding, analysis by, and conversation with Mara Chopping, Rachel Surratt, Misty Heil, Kyria Brown, Josh Kronberg-Rasner, and, especially, Rhett Epler.

Tiantian Zheng would like to thank her Yale advisors Helen Siu, Deborah Davis, William Kelly, and Harold Scheffler for their indefatigable support and inspiration over the past 18 years. She would also like to thank her colleagues at State University of New York, Cortland, for their kind support.

Treena Orchard would like to thank the amazing women who come to My Sister's Place and those who make it the welcoming and vital place it is. Without them, this work would not be possible. These special women include Susan, Cass, Heather, Jenn, Cecilia, Reta, Cary, Bonnie, Christine, Linda, Kim, and the kitchen staff for making good hot meals that she relied on more than once to get her through the day.

Contents

1 Law, Public Policy, and Sex Work in North America and China	1
Legal and Public Policy Responses to Sex Work Cross-Culturally	1
Unintended Consequences? The Impacts of Criminalizing Prostitution	3
Systematic Collusion Within Exclusionary Regimes	5
Ethnographic Context and Methodology	7
Case Study One: China	7
Case Study Two: Canada	12
Case Study Three: The United States	17
Concise Summary Overview of Chapters and Key Arguments	23
References	23
2 Systematic Collusion: Criminalization's Health and Safety Consequences	27
The Impact of Sex Work's Legal Status on Health and Safety	27
Case Study One: China	30
A Violent Working Environment	30
An Exploitative Environment	32
Group Disaffiliation	33
Health Risks	34
Case Study Two: Canada	35
The Impact of Drug User Identity on Health	36
The Impact of Sex Worker Identity on Safety	38
Case Study Three: The United States	40
Restricted Police Aid and Reporting	41
Disrupted Peer Solidarity	42
Limited Information Sharing with Healthcare Providers and Peers	43
Health Diagnosis in Crisis Contexts and the Criminalization of HIV Status	45
Discussion	46
References	48

3 Negotiating Systematic Collusion: Autonomy, Citizenship, and Resistance ... 51
Sex Workers' Negotiations of the Exclusionary Regime ... 51
Case Study One: China ... 54
    Protection Networks ... 54
    Temporary Alliances ... 55
    Contractual Relationships with Regular Clients ... 57
    Urban Citizenship ... 58
Case Study Two: Canada ... 59
    Trying to Engage: Conformity and Avoidance ... 60
    Street-Based Strategies ... 62
Case Study Three: The United States ... 64
    Extrajudicial Problem-Solving and Selective Enlistment of Police Aid ... 65
    Working Independently ... 66
    Work-Related Interpersonal Tool Kit ... 67
    Healthcare during Incarceration or Court-Mandated Addiction Treatment ... 68
Discussion ... 70
References ... 71

4 Researchers' Negotiations of Systematic Collusion ... 75
Ethical Issues in Sex Work Research ... 75
Case Study One: China ... 78
    Negotiating Suspicion ... 78
    Negotiating Violence and Police Raids ... 80
    Negotiating Stigma and Marginalization ... 81
    Negotiating with Scholars in the Academic Field ... 81
Case Study Two: Canada ... 83
    Karma's a Bitch: Negotiating with Regional Radicals ... 83
    The Sex Work "Plan": Negotiating with City Folks ... 86
    Good Help Is Hard to Give ... 88
Case Study Three: The United States ... 88
    Living in Ideals or Living in the World: Taking Sides ... 90
    "Expert Testimony" ... 92
Discussion and Concluding Thoughts ... 94
References ... 95

Index ... 97

About the Authors

Susan Dewey is an applied feminist anthropologist and associate professor of gender and women's studies at the University of Wyoming. She puts her research into practice as the intake coordinator at a Denver transitional housing facility for street-involved women as well as in work she has carried out for UN Women, the US Census Bureau, the International Organization for Migration, and the Wyoming Department of Corrections. She currently leads the Wyoming "Pathways from Prison" action research project with currently and formerly incarcerated women. She is the author or editor of nine books and numerous scholarly articles on sex work, violence against women, and feminized labor. Her most recent book, *Policing Street-Based Prostitution*, will be published by New York University Press in 2017.

Treena Orchard is a medical anthropologist and associate professor in the School of Health Studies at Western University, in London, Ontario. She conducts ethnographic research on sexuality, gender, and health with diverse marginalized populations (i.e., women in sex work, people with HIV/AIDS, Aboriginal groups, gay men, and youth), which she explores through critical medical anthropology, feminist, postcolonial, and political theoretical frameworks. She is the lead researcher on several projects with women in sex work in London, Ontario, and has initiated a new study with women and trans women in sex work in the nearby southern Ontario cities of Kitchener, Waterloo, and Cambridge. Her work has been funded by the Canadian Institutes of Health Research and Western University, and her scholarly articles have appeared in *Social Science & Medicine*; *Culture, Health & Sexuality*; and Sexuality *Research and Social Policy*.

Tiantian Zheng is coauthor of nine books, including *Red Lights: The Lives of Sex Workers in Postsocialist China* and *Ethnographies of Prostitution in Contemporary China*. She is the winner of the 2010 Sara A. Whaley Book Prize from the National Women's Studies Association, and the 2011 Research Publication Book Award from the Association of Chinese Professors of Social Sciences in the United States.

Chapter 1
Law, Public Policy, and Sex Work in North America and China

Legal and Public Policy Responses to Sex Work Cross-Culturally

The state regulation of sexual exchange between consenting adults has long been a contentious subject due to the enduring questions it raises regarding the state's appropriate role in protecting individual rights, status quo social relations, and public health. Legislative and regulatory mechanisms pertaining to transactional sexual exchange[1] inevitably reflect a complex continuum of prevailing cultural beliefs about sociosexual rights, ranging from the right to engage in particular forms of sexual expression in adult consensual relationships to the right to remain free from sexual exploitation. Given the universal importance of these issues, it is unsurprising that the exchange of sex or sexualized intimacy for money or something of value remains a controversial legal and policy issue throughout the world.

Historically and cross-culturally, political calls for the intensified regulation of human sexual expression reflect a gendered sociosexual order that is highly androcentric and privileges the powers and sexual preferences enjoyed by heterosexual men while punishing or otherwise excluding the women[2] who provide paid sexual services to them. Contemporary approaches continue to provide both legislative endorsement of this heterosexual male privilege such as in the form of legislation that mandates testing for sexually transmitted infections among women who sell sex but not their male clients. Globally, approaches that criminalize the purchase of sex

---

[1] Using emic terminology presents challenges when even the use of the phrase "sex work" ignites debates (cf. Farley 2004; Leigh 1997). Hence we refer to "prostitution" when discussing legal regulation, "sex work" when referring to activities described by those engaged in them as labor, and "sex trading" in contexts where women generally regard this activity as the most expedient way to obtain drugs, housing, or money for basic needs, rather than as work.

[2] Men and transgender individuals also engage in transactional sex, but we refer primarily to women throughout this book because of their majority status in the sex industry and because we carried out our research with women.

are often referred to as the "Swedish Model" or the "Nordic Model" as a result of their Scandinavian origins or as "End Demand" because they place male clients under the criminal justice system's purview (Berger 2012). These approaches reflect gendered power imbalances by forcing women to manage clients who, fearing arrest, request sex in more isolated areas that limit women's bargaining power and abilities to protect themselves. Women in the United States face additional challenges as a result of hybrid end demand approaches that feature limited arrests of clients in conjunction with the arrest and court-mandated addictions or other psychological treatment of women involved in prostitution (Wahab and Panichelli 2013). Hence the law remains at best a blunt instrument unable to effectively account for the nuances that characterize transactional sexual encounters in practice.

While a variety of national, state or provincial, and municipal forces govern the sex industry's regulation worldwide, many of these approaches to prostitution can be grouped into the three broad categories of legalization, decriminalization, and criminalization. Governments or municipalities that adopt legalization regard prostitution as a business requiring taxation, licensing, health checks, and zoning to particular locations with police oversight. Legal brothels in Mexico (Kelly 2008), the US state of Nevada (Brents et al. 2009), and the Netherlands, Belgium, and Germany (Weitzer 2011) all operate in this manner and, in keeping with this approach to prostitution as a business, typically require that women working in these locations pay a fee or percentage of their earnings to the owner of the establishment where they work. Government oversight is restrictive in its exclusion of those whose citizenship or health status and gender do not meet licensing or other requirements, which relegates their transactional sexual activities to essentially criminalized conditions where they face police harassment (Katsulis 2008).

Decriminalization involves the removal of laws related to prostitution, while legislation that prohibits abusive practices, such as sex trafficking, remains in place. Notably, countries that have decriminalized prostitution, such as Brazil and New Zealand, often have vibrant sex workers' rights movements that governments and municipalities actively consult in order to promote harm reduction-oriented health and safety measures (Abel et al. 2010; Blanchette and da Silva 2011). De facto decriminalization exists when police opt not to enforce existing laws in particular locales where prostitution is the main economic activity, as in Calcutta's Sonagachi or Bangkok's Patpong (Khruakham and Lawton 2012; Kotiswaran 2014).

Criminalization imposes legal sanctions, which can include incarceration, mandatory psychological treatment, and public registration as a sex offender, on women convicted of prostitution. This approach regards prostitution as a deviant behavior linked to other illegal or socially harmful forces, such as the illicit drug economy and the spread of sexually transmitted infections. Criminalization prevails in the United States, China, Canada, most of Africa and the Middle East, and in some parts of Latin America and Asia, albeit with varying degrees of police surveillance, enforcement, and penalties imposed.[3] The United States, which is

---

[3] The US nonprofit ProCon.org presents a generally well-researched overview of prostitution-related law and policy in 100 countries; we are unable to locate an academic text of such comprehensive scope (http://prostitution.procon.org/view.resource.php?resourceID=000772).

home to the world's most extensive and populous criminal justice system, has enforced criminalization in many locations worldwide via economic sanctions against countries that fail to condemn prostitution (Dewey 2008; Agustín 2007; Mitchell 2011).

The enforcement of anti-prostitution legislation varies by location and often shifts with the tides of political sentiments and yet related policing initiatives consistently and disproportionately affect women who already face significant discrimination because of their ethno-racial identity, citizenship status, or geographic provenance. In many local sexual economies, lighter skinned and more formally educated women generally earn more money by working indoors in situations where they are far less likely to encounter police (Mahdavi 2010). Women who engage in outdoor sex trading, conversely, face a greater likelihood of arrest, detention, and other negative criminal justice encounters due to their high visibility in public space. Since law enforcement practices typically derive from citizen complaints in conjunction with broader municipal, state or provincial, and national priorities, women who face the greatest vulnerabilities while working outdoors also experience the highest arrest rates for prostitution-related offenses.

Unintended Consequences? The Impacts of Criminalizing Prostitution

This book employs a case study approach drawing upon the coauthors' years of ethnographic research with hostess bar workers in China and women engaged in street-based sex trading in Canada and the United States. Our findings illustrate that despite the significant cultural and socioeconomic differences between our field sites, the women in our studies experience similar kinds of systemic harms and social exclusion resulting from the criminalization of sex work. This speaks to the troubling effects of this form of regulation globally and also exposes common areas or domains in which policy makers and social agencies can intervene to better support women in sex work. Research conducted throughout the world demonstrates that criminalizing prostitution has four main negative consequences for women who sell sex: geographical isolation to dangerous areas, increased mistrust of authority figures, further restrictions on housing, employment, and government benefits, and limited possibilities for collective organizing.

First, criminalization forces women to attempt to avoid arrest by working in locales that criminal justice professionals and the women themselves characterize as removed from city centers, poorly lit, industrial or otherwise far from any kind of assistance that women can access in the event of a violent encounter. These areas reduce women's bargaining power with clients and increase their risks of facing assault or even death. Women involved in street-based prostitution also face a high risk of premature death and murder, which includes the significant number of Aboriginal women who are missing or have been murdered, many of whom were involved in the sex trade in different parts of Canada (Brewer et al. 2006; Cameron

2010; Ferris 2015; Quinet 2011; Salfati et al. 2008). Globally, criminalization results in an increased likelihood that a woman who engages in prostitution will experience violence or other human rights violations (Deering, Amin, et al 2014; World Health Organization et al. 2013).

Second, the stigma associated with prostitution results in the women's generalized mistrust of authority figures and negatively compounds their already constrained abilities to obtain healthcare, social services, or report crimes against them to police. Such stigmatizing attitudes significantly impact the lives of women involved in transactional sex by limiting their access to security measures and other supports afforded to citizens who make a living in less socially devalued ways. A direct outcome of this is the denial of or exclusion from healthcare and social services, where women may hesitate to disclose their involvement in transactional sexual activities, which has major implications for women's mental, physical, and sexual health (Andanda 2009; Csete and Cohen 2010; Richter 2013). Another stigma-related outcome is mistrust of authority figures, specifically police, which leads women not to report violence or other incidents against them. This generalized climate of fear and paranoia also increases rates of condomless sex and instances of client or police abuse while also reducing women's abilities to seek necessary services (Kurtz et al. 2005; Shannon et al. 2008).

Third, criminal records for prostitution-related offenses further limit women's abilities to obtain housing, employment, and government benefits that would allow them to change their lives on their own terms, which is particularly significant given that women involved in the most poorly paid and highly policed forms of sexual labor are often the most marginalized. Such exclusion took extreme form until relatively recently in the US state of Louisiana, which mandated public sex offender registration for women convicted of exchanging oral or anal sex for money. New Orleans activist Deon Haywood described this legislation, which prosecutors disproportionately used to convict African-American women, as a "modern-day scarlet letter" (Piano 2011; Dewey and St. Germain 2014). Worldwide, policing procedures that accompany criminalization disproportionately target prostitution in its most visible public forms, which often results in police harassment of the most socioeconomically disadvantaged women (Sanders and Campbell 2014; Simić and Rhodes 2009).

Fourth, the fear of arrest or police scrutiny that accompanies criminalization limits women's solidarity with one another as well as the possibilities for collective rights-based organizing. The members of sex workers' rights movements in countries or locales that criminalize prostitution must constantly negotiate tensions between the risks inherent in public affiliation with illegal activities and the need to advocate for their rights (Crago 2008; Dewey et al. 2013). The sheer heterogeneity of transactional sexual services, significant differences between individuals who perform them, and the divisive environment created by competition for clients, all further restrict possibilities for activist organizing (Zheng 2010). In continuing to exist despite these adversarial forces, sex workers' rights activism constitutes an act of resistance to the exclusionary regimes that shape their lives.

Systematic Collusion Within Exclusionary Regimes

Each of the case studies presented in this book demonstrates that criminalization and its consequences constitute a form of systematic collusion between institutional and social forces that function to socioeconomically marginalize women who engage in transactional sex, particularly prostitution. Criminalization exacts a set of negative totalizing effects on women who sell or trade sex through the operations of an exclusionary regime manifested via criminal justice systems and other state agents, and stigma-related discrimination (Dewey 2014). The exclusionary regime operates with powerful force in the lives of women engaged in criminalized forms of transactional sex in Canada, China, and the United States, all of which embrace a philosophical paradigm that positions prostitution as inherently harmful to both women who engage in it and society more generally. This perspective ignores the complex economic and social forces that, for some women, make sex trading the most appealing and realistic income generation choice from a very constrained menu of options.

Analysis presented throughout this book demonstrates how even well-intentioned law and public policy can have unforeseen consequences, particularly when designed in the absence of any meaningful consultation with those most affected. The judicial systems of all three case study countries rely upon the interpretation of criminal laws informed by a paradoxical premise that positions women who sell or trade sex as both perpetrators of a crime subject to prosecution and victims of an inherently harmful and exploitative situation that no woman would voluntarily choose. This dual positioning of the women as victim criminals has prompted the growth of a judicial–social service alliance in all three countries, such that hostess bar workers in China face detention in rehabilitation camps and women arrested on prostitution-related charges in the United States and Canada regularly must choose between participation in court-mandated treatment programs and incarceration.

While such approaches have deep and complex ideological roots, they are informed by particular kinds of feminist paradigms that position transactional sexual exchange as a form of violence against women. State feminism, which endures in post-socialist China, regards prostitution as a human rights violation that reduces women to the status of objects and commodities. While no official state form of feminism exists in the United States and Canada, policy makers and social agencies that advocate for programs that align with Conservative, neo-abolitionist ideologies have gained significant ascendance in recent years. Yet this translation of particular feminist ideologies into legal practice has resulted in increased risks to the health, safety, and autonomy of women who sell or trade sex.

In China, for instance, police raid health clinics to obtain hostesses' medical records as a means to prosecute them, whereas in the United States some street-involved women avoid emergency room care because they fear that healthcare workers collude with law enforcement officers and social service providers to further restrict their autonomy through arrest, probation, mandatory drug or therapeutic treatment, loss of child custody, or other punitive sanctions. While street-involved women in the United States and Canada face arrest and incarceration on both prostitution- and drug-related charges, US women are more likely to face arrest and receive a jail or prison sentence than their peers in Canada due to the significantly different criminal justice systems in each country.[4] Significantly, street-involved women in the United States and Canada speak in very similar ways about delaying or avoiding contact with healthcare and social service providers due to stigmatizing treatment they receive as women struggling with addictions, mental health issues, and homelessness.

The existence of an exclusionary regime that eschews evidence-based knowledge in favor of morality-based legislation raises numerous ethical and social justice issues for researchers and society at large. We explore the complex means by which state-endorsed exclusionary practices further entrench the inequalities that shape the lives of many women involved in transactional sex in North America and China. Systematic collusion operates in all spheres that relate to transactional sex, and the structure of this book reflects the comprehensively marginalizing impacts of criminalization and its attendant social forces. Chapter 2 explores the complex means by which criminalization negatively impacts the health and safety of women involved in transactional sex, in our respective research sites as well as in other global locations. Importantly, the women do not passively accept this marginalization, and Chapter 3 documents their strategies for resisting and negotiating within sociolegal systems that alternately target them as victims, agents of contagion, and criminal perpetrators who disregard the law. Chapter 4 engages with researchers' negotiations of and resistance against systematic collusion and in so doing addresses the challenges that accompany research in a politically and ethically fraught field.

As feminist anthropologists conducting research in and writing about our home communities, we share a deep political commitment to working against the exclusionary forces that destroy the lives and communities of the women we have come to know and care deeply about. Zheng[5] conducts research in Dalian, the Northeastern Chinese city in which she was born and lived before moving to the United States and to which she returns yearly. Orchard lives in the London, Ontario neighborhood where she carries out her research and often does not distinguish the boundaries between her work in "the field" from her life at home. Dewey works as a service provider at a Denver transitional housing facility for women leaving the sex industry and provides confidential harm reduction counseling and referrals on a twenty-four hour basis through the anonymous helpline she created and also conducts weekly visits to women who are working the streets, escorting, or incarcerated in jail or prison.

---

[4] While street-involved women in Canada regularly face arrest and detention, the sheer enormity of the US criminal system results in a greater likelihood that street-involved women in the United States will face incarceration following an arrest. US jails and prisons currently house 2.24 million people, not including individuals under other forms of correctional control such as probation, parole, or other court-mandated oversight. The United States holds more than a quarter of the world's prisoners despite comprising just 5 % of the global population, with the Chinese population of sentenced prisoners, at 1.6 million, comprising the second largest population of incarcerated persons (Walmsley 2013). Statistics Canada, in contrast, reports just 38,219 incarcerated adults (Statistics Canada 2010/2011).

[5] Zheng's sections in this book include a rewritten, altered version of certain sections from *Red Lights* (University of Minnesota Press 2009).

We see firsthand, as a result of our ethnographic engagement and shared community membership, the oppressive and sometimes deadly toll that criminalization exacts upon the women. We have all known women through our work, and the friendships that often emerged from it, who as a result of their involvement in criminalized activities could not enlist police or social service support even when they desperately needed it. Our long-term association with the women has led us to understand that the complexities and contradictions inherent in their everyday lives do not lend themselves to easy solutions. Very few of the women we have worked with describe their transactional sexual activities as anything more than a means to make a living or meet basic needs. As the case studies below clearly demonstrate, the criminalization of their income generating activities functions comprehensively and effectively to ensure their further marginalization from social assistance mechanisms and society more generally.

Ethnographic Context and Methodology

Case Study One: China

Ethnographic Context

Dalian

Dalian is a booming metropolitan seaport city at the southern tip of Liaoning Peninsula in Northeastern China. The city has a unique colonial history, previously occupied by czarist Russia in 1898 and then by the Japanese from 1905 until 1945. During the colonial period, sex work in Dalian was an integral part of the entertainment industry, and the separation of courtesans' residences, entertainment hotels, and brothels was a unique feature of sex work in the city. Courtesans who lived in separate quarters met their customers in entertainment hotels to converse, sing, and play music, and then often moved on to brothels to enjoy food and sex.

The Japanese occupation in 1937 introduced another category of sex work to the city in the form of "comfort women," local women captured by Japanese troops for use as sex slaves. After the anti-Japanese war ended, the city was politically liberated by the Community Party and reincorporated into China. Maoist Dalian (1949–1976) allegedly eradicated sex work, partly by enforcing the rural–urban divide, stripping peasants of all mobility and exploiting peasants to support and serve the need of city residents. While the Maoist isolation of peasants in the countryside impeded the flow of sex workers, it laid the foundation for the resurgence of sex work in the 1980s and 1990s.

During the post-Mao era, in 1984, Dalian was granted the status of "special economic zone" (SEZ), following the other economically developed cities of Shenzhen, Zhuhai, Shantou, and Xiamen, that had benefited from the more liberal economic policies associated with the status of SEZ. By the late 1990s, Dalian had grown exponentially from a fishing village in the nineteenth century to a metropolis with a population of 6.7 million. Known as "Hong Kong of the North" and "Pearl in the

North," Dalian's rapid growth has made it a magnet for rural migrants seeking employment in the city. In the 1980s during the post-Mao period, it was the desperate poverty that drove peasants to break the floodgates and fill the cities in China with an estimated six million sex workers in 2003 (Tucker et al. 2011).

The Karaoke Bar Entertainment Industry

While commodity consumption was strictly regulated and politicized to ensure the egalitarian ideology during the Maoist era, the post-Mao market economy's pro-consumption policy unleashed a proliferation of nightclubs and karaoke bars. In Dalian, karaoke bars can be found almost every few steps throughout the city. During my research in the city, the city's police chief told me that Dalian was home to 4000 nightclubs, saunas, and karaoke bars. Sexual services take place in these entertainment establishments that not only include karaoke bars, saunas, and nightclubs but also stretch to hotels, hair salons, disco and other dance halls, small roadside restaurants, parks, movie houses, and video rooms.

Among these establishments that provide sexual services, karaoke bars represent the high-end service that demand the most stringent criteria for women's height, facial beauty, figure, and social skills such as singing, dancing, flirting, drinking, and conversation. Unlike many other establishments that provide nothing but sexual intercourse, karaoke bar hostesses are chosen by male clients as company for the night for their beauty and skills in a host of services such as singing, dancing, and conversations. Karaoke bar hostesses often charge twice as much for sexual services as those in other establishments. Patrons to these new consumption sites are mainly middle-aged entrepreneurs, government officials, policemen, and foreign investors. They can purchase the services of hostesses for their business partners to secure relationships and broker business deals with their business partners and patrons in the government.

Hostesses or escorts who engage in the male-centered rituals of business and politics are called "*sanpei xiaojie*," literally, "young women who accompany men in three ways" and a euphemism for "sex workers." These three ways can be all encompassing, including alcohol consumption, dancing, singing, caressing, and sexual services. These women are often 17–23 years of age. Of the 200 hostesses with whom I worked, only 4 came from cities and the rest were rural migrant women. Institutional constraints via the household registration policy and social discrimination have made the vast majority of rural migrants work in the lowest rung of the labor market, such as construction workers, garbage collectors, restaurant waitresses, domestic maids, and factory workers. During my research, I was told by the police chief that 80 % of the rural migrant women came to work as hostesses or sex workers. Although he may be exaggerating, his estimate did demonstrate that a substantial percentage of migrant women worked as sex workers.

I conducted fieldwork in ten karaoke bars in total, but focused most of my time and energy on three bars of, respectively, high, medium, and low status. The criterion of the hierarchy of the bars is based on the location of the bar, organization, management, the level of hostesses' physical attractiveness, and consumption standards.

Here I will mainly discuss the low-tier bar setting, which corresponds more closely with the US and Canada case studies presented in this book. The low-tier bar "Romantic Dream" was located in the red light district that was infamous for the dirty environment and aggressive men engaged in criminalized activities. This red light district comprised a line of 26 karaoke bars in a decaying neighborhood clustered underneath an operating railroad in Shahekou district. First built in 1996, this red light district street was plagued by violence, with residents finding dead bodies lying on the street almost every morning for the first 3 years of its existence, until police crackdowns reduced the endemic gang-related violence in this area.

I was told that government officials were secretly connected with these gangsters who were street fighters and belonged to a number of criminal organizations. Throughout the red light district, gangsters either worked as owners and bouncers of karaoke bars and disco bars or came to visit the area. During my fieldwork there, I witnessed many fierce, bloody fights, and saw gangsters roaming around the area, often times beating or raping hostesses, plundering bars, and selling drugs, such as ketamine powder, ecstasy, and other illicit substances in entertainment venues.

Romantic Dream offered services provided by 27 hostesses. Upon entry into the bar, one could immediately see the hostesses in the hallway, sitting on the couch watching television or applying makeup to their faces. The first floor housed 20 karaoke rooms, and the second floor consisted of a waiters' dorm, hostesses' dorm, and a room for sexual encounters. At Romantic Dream, the prices of snacks, fruit plates, and hostesses' tips were all negotiable. The bar owner bought the barkeeper's freedom from prison after he had been sentenced to death for killing several men in a fight, and his presence scared many gangsters and others who might cause trouble away from the bar.

Policing and Regulating Sex Work

Maoist China enforced an abolitionist policy, which postsocialist China continues to support, that allegedly eliminated sex work in China. Over the past decades, China has released a proliferation of legislation that outlaws sex work and third party involvement in sex work. Such an abolitionist approach holds that no women would voluntarily choose sex work because it commodifies and humiliates women by stripping women of their legal rights and prohibiting women's advancement in society. Because the Chinese government purports that women would not choose a profession that violates their own human rights, these laws are designed to target those who engage in third party organization of sex work, illicit sexual relations with sex workers, and trafficking.

These series of laws include the first criminal Law in 1979, the 1987 Regulations, the 1984 Criminal Law, the 1991 Decision on Strictly Forbidding the Selling and Buying of Sex, the 1991 Decision on the Severe Punishment of Criminals Who Abduct and Traffic in or Kidnap Women and Children, the 1992 Law on Protecting the Rights and Interests of Women (Women's Law), the Revised Criminal Law of 1997, and the 1999 Entertainment Regulations. The 1986 Regulations promulgated that it is forbidden to sell and purchase sex, to introduce others into sex work, and to offer accommodation for sex work. The 1997 Criminal Law states that those who organize or force others into sex work will be sentenced to between 5 and 10 years' imprisonment or, in serious cases, life imprisonment or the death penalty.

The Public Security Bureau enforces these laws through police raids led as part of "crackdowns," campaigns that last for about 3 months at a time to be repeated three times a year, strategically centering on important holidays such as National Day and Army Day and events such as the APEC conference. The Public Security Bureau utilizes a complex system to attack and raid karaoke bars using techniques they describe as "guerrilla warfare" (*da youji*), co-opting the term used to describe the heroic efforts of the Communist revolutionaries against the Japanese invaders and Nationalists. Raids come in different forms: regular raids and shock raids, timed raids and random raids, systematic raids and block raids, daytime raids and night raids. Performance of the unit and individuals is measured in the number of arrested hostesses and amount of fines they are able to collect from sex workers, for which they receive bonuses and honor from the municipal government (Zheng 2009a). These police raids are often times unannounced, sudden, unexpected, and large scale, and take place in addition to more mundane policing that takes place when plain-clothed policemen pose as customers at these establishments, seeking evidence to arrest sex workers.

Each police raid usually results in arrests and detention of hostesses and severe fines. During my research, many hostesses I worked with were arrested by the police. Each of them had to submit a fine up to 5000 yuan ($833) in order to be released. Unless they turned in the fine, they would be detained at labor camps where, in the name of rehabilitation, they would serve 6 months to 2 years. It is worth noting that this amount of fine continued to be the same in the massive police raids in 2010, though in some cities it went as high as 10,000 yuan (US$1667) (Pan and Huang 2011). It was also imperative for bar owners to regularly submit bribes to the police, hoping for either exemption from or information about impending police raids. The process of determining sex workers' guilt, penalty, fines, and punishment was, and continues to be, handled single-handedly by the police without the involvement of the courts or criminal justice system.

In implementing state policy, the police often times appropriate these laws for their own benefits through extortion from both hostesses and bar owners. Because the police harbor the arbitrary power to arrest and fine hostesses, hostesses are extremely terrified when they are chosen by plain-clothed police. In such instances, hostesses have no alternative but to obey the demands of the police including sexual services, and in some instances police officials keep hostesses as part of their personal harem in exchange for immunity from police arrests and fines.

Methodology

I conducted 24 cumulative months of fieldwork in Dalian between 1999 and 2003 and an updated research on sex work in China in 2015. My research sample includes around 200 bar hostesses in ten karaoke bars, although I was most intensely involved with three karaoke bars in which I worked as a hostess myself while living with the hostesses in the low-tier bar. Initially every bar owner I talked to rejected my initial attempts to conduct research in karaoke bars, but eventually I made friends with a government official, who introduced me to these karaoke bars. Bar owners introduced me to the hostesses as a university student coming from the United States to do research and write a book on their lives. Hostesses, in general, appeared nonchalant toward the owners' introductory remarks. Some found it hard to comprehend why anyone would be interested in studying them as they described themselves as "nobodies."

My first attempts to interact with hostesses were unsuccessful; when I tried starting a conversation with a hostess sitting next to me, she stood up and left me in the cold. Although I was sitting among the hostesses, I felt alienated, as each of them riveted their eyes on the incoming clients and prepared themselves for selection by the clients. When they did get a chance to look at me, they mocked my student attire, my glasses, and my inability to understand or participate in their sex talks and jokes. They nicknamed me "glasses" and "college student," which further marked me as a complete outsider. When they questioned how I could financially sustain my research, I honestly told them about the research grant that I received; they shook their heads and determined that I would never be able to understand their struggles for survival.

I also noticed that hostesses were extremely wary of potential assaults or betrayals by police, gangsters, and each other since police planted "spy hostesses" to inform on other hostesses' sex work activities in exchange for self-protection. These potential risks made it imperative that every hostess kept her identity secret from each other. In the bars, they knew each other by a pseudonym, a fake hometown, and a life story that they invented. Due to these hurdles, I came to realize that this research would be impossible if I remained an outsider in their eyes. The only way for me to be transformed from an outsider to an insider was to work with them, live with them, and learn from them. Through participating in their work and lives, I would be able to not only observe and experience everything they do but also work with them as colleagues and friends with shared experiences, emotion, and feelings. Upon this realization, I submitted the living accommodation fees to the low-tier bar owner, and from then on, I lived and worked with the hostesses in the bar and became intensely involved in every aspect of their lives.

In the bar, we typically ordered dinner around 6, when customers started trickling into the bar. We sat together in the bar lobby watching television, videos, and chatting, while waiting to enter the bar in order to be selected by the customers as the company for the evening. Around midnight, we ordered breakfast, and went to bed around 3 in the morning. During the daytime, we ordered a meal from a nearby restaurant and went shopping or visiting hair salons or beauty parlors. Living and working with hostesses built trust between hostesses and me and drew us together. We shared the same dangers, bitterness, and jokes about our hostessing experiences, and as time went by, we became close friends who relied on each other in our everyday lives in the bar, a relationship that was far beyond the researcher–subject relationship.

Hostesses confided in me about their personal problems, relationship problems, and family issues with their parents. In helping them and offering a different perspective, I became a part of their lives and befriended their boyfriends, regular clients, parents, family members, and friends. I followed two hostesses back to their rural hometowns and lived in each of these rural places for several months. Familiarity with the people in their social networks helped me corroborate stories told by the hostesses with stories told by their friends, boyfriends, regular clients, family members, and parents (see Dewey and Zheng 2013, p. 33).

Living and working with hostesses also offered me a chance to learn professional advice from them, such as the techniques to thwart clients' sexual advances. Despite these precautions and techniques, I still became embroiled in conflicts with clients at times and relied upon hostesses and bar owners to support and help me. On one occasion a client asked me to go with him to a teahouse to have tea at 2 in the morning, and remained tenacious and persistent when I declined. A hostess in the karaoke room, foreseeing an impending conflict, went out and called in the bar manager, who negotiated with the customer while I escaped into the back of the bar. Hostesses warned me that I could be raped by the customer if I went out with him and advised me to leave the bar for a while, which I did. After walking aimlessly in the city for a couple of hours, I called the bar to check if the customer had left. The bar manager told me that the customer had waited two hours for me to return before the bar bouncer forced him out.

I combined participant observation experiences in three bars with extended visits to two hostesses' rural hometowns, as well as open-ended and semi-structured interviews with people inside and outside of bars. These included the bar owners and managers, madams, bar hostesses, bar bouncers, police officers, government officials, male clients, retired hostesses, hostesses' parents, family members, village residents, and urban people from all walks of life. Taken together, this broad ethnographic lens helped me to formulate a complex portrait of hostesses' equally complex lives.

Case Study Two: Canada

Ethnographic Context

London

Historically inhabited by the Attawandaron, Algonquin, and Haudenosaunee First Nations, London was established in 1793 as part of the British Colony of Upper Canada by Lieutenant Colonel John Simcoe (Cunningham 1976; Miller 1988). Originally selected as an administrative center for the burgeoning British Empire, London developed into a modern city during the nineteenth century with the expansion of agriculture and industrial development (i.e., oil refinery, steel foundries). Its strategic position alongside national and local railway systems also made it a central player in the distribution and trade of various goods in the region. Today London is Canada's 11th largest city with a population of approximately 375,000 and is recognized as an important center of commerce, post-secondary education (2 universities and several colleges), healthcare, and manufacturing.

London has been very hard hit by successive economic recessions in the region that began in the 1990s, particularly the global outsourcing of manufacturing that has contributed to higher rates of unemployment (10 %) compared to the provincial average (7 %). Other indicators of socioeconomic disparity in the city include the rising numbers of lone, primarily female-headed households (18 %), those living on social assistance (17 %), and the fact that 20 % of children in the city live in poverty (Statistics Canada 2006). A closer look at the city's poorest residents reveals even more troubling forms of marginalization, particularly in the disadvantaged and stigmatized East of Adelaide neighborhood, where the street-based sex work and thriving drug trade economies are predominantly located.

East of Adelaide

What is known today as the "East of Adelaide" neighborhood began as an independent farming and industry town, which was annexed to become part of the growing City of London in 1885. The *East of Adelaide* or *London East* neighborhood bears the marks of a community left behind in the wake of contemporary economic change and civic development, including factory and local service industry closures and reduced social as well as health infrastructure to support the neighborhood's residents; particularly the large number of poor people living here. While these hallmarks of neoliberalism affect many residents of the city, they impact the already disadvantaged residents in East of Adelaide particularly hard. Unemployment is higher (12 % for men and 8 % for women) here than in other parts of the city (around 7 %), as are rates of home rentals, lone-parent households, and many individual income levels hover just above the poverty line ($20,000 for a single person). Many First Nations people call this area home and although they constitute just 1.9 % of the city's population, they are over-represented in the homeless and prison populations, and more women, men, and children from these groups live in poverty compared to others in the city (City of London 2011).

In the media and mainstream social discourse this part of London and those who call it home are often represented through tropes of despair, danger, and cultural irrelevance compared to more prosperous areas of the city, often through reference to the "area's persistent problems with drugs and prostitution" (Gillespie 2011). However, among local residents and those interested in gentrification opportunities competing narratives about this community circulate, as a proud, historic, working class, artistic place where people watch out for and take care of one another. From my on-going ethnographic observations and community involvement in the neighborhood, it is all of the above: a place of grinding poverty, addictions,[6] street-based

---

[6] Injection drug use is extremely high in London and over one million syringes are distributed each year through the Regional HIV/AIDS Connection (RHAC). Despite the stigmatizing image of the East of Adelaide neighborhood as the main "drug scene," RHAC employees distribute safe injection materials to users throughout London, including the suburbs and economically wealthy areas.

sex work, and marginalization; a place populated with people who are trying to survive while being excluded from participation in mainstream economic opportunities; a place of heavy police surveillance; and a place that offers varying degrees of social and health services for those who call the area home. One of my participants described her feelings about the community and the solidarity as well as mutual respect that exists among people on the neighborhood's streets:

> I'm off the streets. I just like the people on the street...It's like I got a special spot in my heart, man. You know, I mean, how can you not help them people?...I just get sucked into coming down here and walking down the street and talking to some of them, you know... Most people with anything to offer in life, have been street people, for me. But, you know what I mean? Yeah, they're just so talented and so special.

The Regulation of Sex Work

Until recently the regulatory approach to sex work in Canada was that of quasi-criminalization, and while sex work itself was legal all of the activities related to doing sex work were illegal. The three laws used to criminalize those in the sex trade were those pertaining to communicating for the purposes of sex work, keeping and being found in a common bawdy house, and living off of the avails of sex work. In 2007, Ontario sex workers Terri Jean Bedford, Valerie Scott, and Amy Lebovitch challenged these laws on the basis that they pose significant threats to sex trade workers' health, security, and human rights (Bunch 2014). Known as *Bedford V Canada*, this case has moved through the Ontario Superior Court to the highest court in Canada—the Supreme Court of Canada. At both of these legislative levels the judgments have favored the plaintiffs and the laws were deemed unconstitutional as well as harmful to people in sex work (Lawrence 2015).

However, on June 4 of 2014 the ruling Conservative party forced through *Bill C-36 Protection of Communities and Exploited Persons Act*, which usurps the landmark decisions of *Bedford V Canada* and includes new criminalizing provisions. Not only are the three laws that were deemed unconstitutional back on the books, for the first time in Canadian history the purchase of sex is now illegal, as is advertising for sexual services. Upon the passing of Bill C-36 the federal justice minister also announced 20 million dollars of new funding for social service providers to encourage and support people to leave the sex industry. The messages communicated through this bill and its attendant "abolitionist-friendly" funding are frightening and resurrect debased stereotypes about sex trade workers as dangerous criminals who need to be saved, and they also open up many new opportunities for increased violence, poverty, and social dispossession among those who depend upon sex work to survive (Benoit et al. 2014; Bruckert 2002).

In many cities across Canada, including London, the exact approach to take regarding the policing and regulation of sex work is uncertain given the vociferous debates about this new prospective law and sex work in general, which has divided service providers on the issue and left women and others in the trade in the balance. That many women have little to no knowledge about these changes to the laws that powerfully govern their lives is also problematic, and I discuss this in more detail in Chapter 2.

Methodology

This was a joint project with Susan Dewey and the local agency which has been my community partner on all of my sex work studies in London, My Sister's Place (MSP). The objectives were to comparatively explore healthcare, social services, and criminal justice from the perspectives of women in sex work and professionals working in these fields in Canada and the United States. I conducted 35 interviews in total, 22 with women in sex work and 13 with different service providers who work closely with this population across the areas of health, social services, and criminal justice. I also took field notes during the project, which were handwritten in a notebook. The interviews with the women were conducted from May to July of 2014 and those with the providers were done between August and November of 2014.

Interviews with Women in Sex Work

Each semi-structured interview, which ran between 30 and 90 minutes and was tape-recorded, took place in a private room or office at MSP. The women were recruited with the assistance of several MSP staff, who suggested suitable prospective participants, and we[7] also had a poster up at the agency with a description of the study and my contact information. Although I began the first few interviews using an interview guideline identical to Dewey's, I found it uncomfortable to refer to questions on a piece of paper during the interview and opted for a more free-flowing, life-history kind of discussion. I knew a number of the women from my previous project; however, at least half of our sample of 22 women were new to me.

Socio-Demographic Profile of the Women

The age range of our participants was between 28 and 63, with the majority being middle age or around 41. With respect to racial and/or cultural identity, most women were White ($n=14$), followed by Aboriginal ($n=6$), Mixed ancestry ($n=2$), and Black ($n=1$). Interestingly, only five of our participants grew up in London and the majority are from other southern Ontario towns or cities, 11/22 and 3/22, respectively. Two participants were from other Canadian provinces and one woman is from the United States. Given that so few women are from London I asked what brought them to the city, and the primary reasons were having family or friends in the city, moving with boyfriends, the drug scene, and medical services (primarily methadone). For many of our participants, London is not their favorite place to live because it is a small city, rather conservative, and some of the monikers used by our participants capture its less than vital nature: the "armpit of the world" and "Lucifer's rejects."

---

[7] Throughout this section and all others authored by me, I use "we" most often when referring to my work in London because although I conducted the interviews this project is very much a joint effort, a collaborative labor of love between myself and all the staff at MSP.

With respect to the women's experiences within the sex work spectrum, they have all at one time or another participated in various indoor and privately arranged situations prior to or alongside their street-based work. However, street-based work is what women have done for the longest period of time, and that is what they focused on in their interviews. The majority are still working to support their addictions, to survive, and because sex work and the local street scene in which it is embedded constitutes the heart of the women's socioeconomic and familial worlds.

Interviews with Service Providers

All of the service provider interviews, with the exception of one,[8] were semi-structured, individual discussions conducted at their workplace or a locale of their choosing. The interviews were designed to learn how providers approach their work with women in sex work, the key challenges they experience in this work, the main barriers they see in the women's lives that prevent them from getting the kinds of help they need, and suggestions for ways to streamline, improve, or better coordinate the services offered.

Seven interviews were conducted with providers in the broad domain of social services, including three at MSP, one at a sexual assault center, one at a local neighborhood resource center, and two at a community agency designed to help women and others in the street culture secure housing. Five interviews were done with professionals in the medical or health-related fields, including two at an HIV/AIDS agency, one nurse practitioner who works extensively with women in sex work, one at a domestic violence program in a local hospital, and one at a community health center that specializes in providing healthcare to street-involved populations. I also did one interview with a woman working in the field of criminal justice, who does outreach with and advocates for women in sex work. She works at a charitable agency that has adopted a restorative justice stance versus a purely punitive approach in their work with marginalized populations, which she described in the following way:

> Allowing people to accept responsibility for any criminal act that they might have done and what the harms are to the community. But also giving them an opportunity to grow beyond that and not be identified in that, as that is what's defined them. So, it's moving, it's moving on.

Capturing the Field

The following excerpt from my field notes are from a meeting I attended at MSP, the transitional support agency for women that I have worked with in my on-going research with women in sex work in the city since 2010 (Orchard et al. 2012, 2013, 2014; Orchard 2015). The meeting was about developing a pamphlet to improve services for women in sex work and some more general observations at MSP. They

---

[8] One interview was conducted with two staff members at a local needle exchange, and their preference was to do the interview together.

capture the feel of the agency, the interactions between the women, and some of the challenges related to finding ways to help and better serve women in sex work.

"An important set of issues was raised with respect to the implications of police zoning of the women, which totally determines where they can and cannot go/be. It is often the central areas of Dundas and Hamilton Rd. where they are zoned, alternately, which cuts them off from so many aspects/people/services/work/dope that they depend upon. When they need to go to court and are zoned from the downtown area they are screwed and can be picked up on a violation or breach. Many women don't have a social or caseworker who could help them access services or bring the services to them versus always putting the onus on the women to come to them. We need service consolidation, including for those who are getting out of detention centers and jail. As one woman said 'a bus pass to nowhere isn't enough.'

Many women access some services when in detention centers but when they get out, they've lost everything because they were in jail (housing, possessions, access to methadone and other treatments, relationships, Ontario Works, Ontario Disability Support Program). They end up back on the street. An address is essential for support, getting back on OW and so many things. The Salvation Army allows women to use their address, but they often use an address of a friend and those offering the place take a cut from their check. Some women don't want to be involved in the system at all and just get into the street scene. There isn't enough transitional support between incarceration and the street. The church people do help but their work only goes so far and has strings. The pamphlet should be about what women are having problems with, safety issues, what services and people they need to connect to.

While waiting for interviews, I spoke with the woman beside me: blunt bob, red lipstick, cool colored square glasses. She spoke about being sick and then said "oh, there she is, big mouth" or something. She was referring to that older, skinny woman with a few front teeth…She and someone else were starting something at lunch—mainly about being ripped off. The woman beside me said the troublesome one always starts shit and should be asked to either leave or clean toilets for 6 months! She added that one of the problems is that she gets rewarded for her bad behavior, and her behavior sets off or triggers other women.

As I was heading home, I saw Alex by the bus stop and she yelled out a couple of times 'anyone want to buy a bus pass?'"

Case Study Three: The United States

Ethnographic Context

Denver, Colorado

Gold prospectors first camped on Arapaho and Cheyenne tribal land in 1851, and, in 1858, these and other settlers named the Rocky Mountain foothills near the Platte River "Denver," in honor of the then-current Kansas Territorial Governor (Landry

2013; Leonard and Noel 1991). Lucrative oil, gas, and mineral extractive industries,[9] combined with the outdoor tourism sector and large-scale agricultural production, have all directly contributed to Denver's enjoyment of higher than US national average growth rates for the past eight decades (Metro Denver Economic Development Corporation 2015). Denver is the largest city in the US Southwest and, with a metropolitan area population of 2.9 million,[10] is home to over half of all Colorado residents (US Census Bureau 2012). Denverites self-identify as 70 % White, 32 % Hispanic (including those who self-identify as "White"), 10 % African-American, 2.8 % Asian, and 1.3 % Native American, and the city has higher than national average rates of home ownership (52.5 %) and formal education, with 84 % of city residents holding a B.A. degree or higher (US Census Bureau 2012).

Both despite and because of this general affluence, Northern Colorado has a decades-old affordable housing shortage (Murray 2002, p. 286). Denver's Road Home Program, which is part of the Denver City Council's 10 year plan to end homelessness, estimates the number of Denver residents who have experienced homelessness over the past 3 years at between 8315 and 6204, with an additional 2230 precariously housed; women constitute slightly less than half of this population (Metro Denver Homelessness Initiative 2014, pp. vii–viii). Like their housed peers, many people experiencing homelessness use drugs, and sometimes addiction and related mental health issues intersect with individuals' difficulties in finding and keeping stable housing.

This echoes results from my sample of 131 street-involved women who sought services at a transitional housing facility for women leaving sex work. The women self-identified as struggling with addictions to the following substances: cocaine and its derivatives (51 % among single substance users, 38 % of polysubstance users), alcohol (16 % of single substance users, with no polysubstance users self-identifying problematic usage), and methamphetamine (13 % among single substance users, 19 % among polysubstance users). These findings generally confirm citywide data on illicit substance use collected by a division of the Denver Department of Human Services (Denver Office of Drug Strategy 2012).

East Colfax Avenue

Denver street-based prostitution and illicit drug economies intersect, as in many US cities, with women exchanging sex for money or drugs in the same location where they live, use drugs, and solicit clients. This totalizing environment, in which street-involved women spend most of their time, features high levels of violence according to both women's own accounts and police statistics (Denver Police Department

---

[9] Historical research on sex work in Denver clearly underscores the connections between an early economy fuelled by almost exclusively male resource extraction industries and the growth of sex work (Butler 1986; MacKell 2009, 2007).

[10] This population includes those who live in Adams, Arapahoe, Boulder, Broomfield, Denver, Douglas, and Jefferson Counties.

2015). During my participant observation in the East Colfax Avenue neighborhood, where most street-based sex trading takes place, the women and I routinely witnessed physical altercations, shouting matches, and, less frequently, gun violence, all of which would rapidly cause the streets to empty as people returned to their motel rooms or other concealed locations to await the inevitable arrival of police sirens. Despite this socioeconomic strife, "the fax," as Denver residents refer to it, is a cultural space of transgression similar to many neighborhoods throughout the world known for high levels of sex work-related activities, celebrated for its bohemian nature as well as for its resilient inhabitants.

Colfax Avenue is one of the longest streets in the United States, spanning 26 miles through Denver and the surrounding towns of Aurora, Denver, Lakewood, and Golden. Local reporters and bloggers frequently mention that *Playboy* magazine once characterized this street, called "Golden Road" before being renamed after an Indiana Congressperson, as "the longest, wickedest street in America." In an attempt to capture this street's popular cultural significance in the Denver area and Rocky Mountain region more generally, I used this phrase to conduct a Google search and received hundreds of results from sources as varied as the Denver Public Library, countless independent blogs and sites, a self-published book series entitled *Denver After Dark*, and *Crossing Colfax*, a short story collection by local authors. The street also features prominently in serious literature, including in Jack Kerouac's *On the Road*, where the author drinks, carouses, and saves a friend from assault in the street's many bars and related establishments (Kerouac 1957, p. 37, 45–46, 11, 257–258).

Colfax.com, a Web site that celebrates the street's notoriety while promoting neighborhood music and cultural events, has sponsored a "Miss Colfax" pin-up contest since 2007 which features monthly amateur photographs of scantily clad women. The general health and elaborate lingerie and makeup worn by the women in the photographs indicate that they are most likely not street involved, and yet their sexualized poses indicate that the women (and the site's organizers) hope to capitalize on the presence of large number of street-involved women in the area; notably, the single comment at the end of this page reads "that's a lot of hookers on one page!" ("Miss Colfax" 2014).

The site's mid-century pin-up girl reference draws upon Colfax Avenue's history as a major interstate thoroughfare for post-World War II tourists prior to the construction of Interstate 70. In 1958, the Colorado Visitors Bureau listed 43 motels on West Colfax Avenue and 50 on East Colfax in addition to dozens of gas stations, auto parts stores, and restaurants, and by 1990, 60 % of the motels still operated on East Colfax and 42 % on West Colfax (Wyckoff 1992, pp. 285–286). Increased policing of the Capitol Hill neighborhood, the location of the gold-domed Colorado State Capitol building in downtown Denver, beginning in the early 1970s dispersed the illicit sex and drug trades to the eastern and western extremities of Colfax Avenue, where these motels served as a convenient place for the women to live and work (Wyckoff 1992, p. 289). With grandiose names like The Niagara, The Aristocrat, and The Riviera, motels that previously functioned as vacation retreats for touring middle class families today serve as the primary sites for the women's illicit drug and transactional sexual exchanges.

Policing and Regulating the Sex Trade

Denver's prostitution-related legislation and public policy began to receive US national attention in 1994 following the instigation of one of the first end demand initiatives targeting sex workers' clients. This initiative mandated that clients pay a $1000 fine that was in turn used to purchase newspaper space to publish pictures of men arrested for approaching women they believed to be sex workers (Dodge et al. 2005). East Colfax Avenue is located in the Denver Police Department's District Six, where, as in other districts, policing priorities, citizen complaints, and individual behavior all play critical determining roles in a woman's likelihood of facing arrest on a given day.

Officers typically arrest a woman on a prostitution-related charge[11] after witnessing behaviors associated with this legal offense, such as repeatedly entering cars or motel rooms with different men, hailing male passersby, and even spending extended periods of time on the street. Women also face arrest in undercover operations, in which a plainclothes officer obtains sufficient evidence to make an arrest following a woman's statement of a particular sex act's price. After gathering evidence in one of these ways, the arresting officer tells the woman that she is under arrest on prostitution-related charges and reads her the Miranda warning, which informs her of the right to remain silent and of the criminal justice system's right to use her subsequent statements as evidence against her.

This encounter evolves very rapidly from a woman's agreement to, or engagement in, a sex act in exchange for money to a situation in which she faces incarceration for a minimum of 1 month. In many cases, women can receive sentences of a year or more depending on their history of criminal convictions, outstanding warrants, and the jurisdiction in which the arrest occurs. Ensuing events will take multiple trajectories determined by these factors, all of which the arresting officer can quickly ascertain through records obtained electronically or via radio contact while the woman is handcuffed in the back of the squad car. While transporting the woman to a district station holding cell where she will stay until booked into county jail, the arresting officer may decide to question her regarding information she might have about more powerful street-involved figures. This decision will likely stem from the officer's assessment of her knowledge based upon what the officer ascertains from her criminal record or, in some cases, previous contact with her.

Hence a woman can find herself quickly transformed from a person facing a potential criminal conviction to a potential informant in a criminal case against a prominent figure in the illicit drug or sex economy. Street-involved women are often ideal informants due to their connections to illicit drug markets both as consumers and as sexual partners to men who play active roles in producing, distributing, and enforcing order in this economy, as well as prostitution's low status as a misdemeanor offense akin to loitering. In instances where a police officer asks a woman to volunteer information with the potential to avoid incarceration or receive a

---

[11] For a complete list of all Colorado Statutes related to prostitution extant at the time of the research, see Morris et al. (2012) (Appendix B, pp. 97–103).

reduced sentence, she must rapidly weigh the consequences of going to jail or possibly facing retribution from a street-involved figure she may provide information about. The effects of controlled substances considerably mitigate the circumstances in which a woman makes these potentially life-changing choices, as do sleep deprivation, and other factors that compromise her decision making.

Generally a woman arrested on prostitution-related charges will spend less than 12 hours in a holding cell, followed by her transfer to booking in the county jail, where she will be photographed and provided with a uniform while she awaits her court date, which typically takes place within 2 weeks. Women fortunate enough to have friends or family members with sufficient economic resources to post bail may leave jail at this point until they return for their court hearing, but most women's struggles with homelessness and addiction render them indigent and unable to mobilize such assistance. At the time of their court date, most women receive a public defender who reviews their case and meets them for the first time minutes before standing in front of the judge.

A woman may choose to speak directly to the judge during the few minutes that precede her sentencing or opt instead to allow her public defender to communicate any extenuating circumstances that surrounded her prostitution arrest. Sentencing for a prostitution-related conviction typically comprises 30, 60, or 90 days, yet a number of factors inform judicial decision-making in prostitution-related cases, including consideration of a woman's struggles with addiction, her previous record of arrests and convictions, and her HIV status. A woman charged with a prostitution-related offense, or a public defender speaking on her behalf, may choose to inform the judge that she only engages in transactional sex as a result of her addiction to a controlled substance.

The judge weighs this inform in conjunction with her previous record of arrests and criminal convictions and then imposes a sentence. A woman with no criminal record may receive only probation and a fine, whereas a woman with a lengthy list of convictions could spend a year in county jail, sometimes in a special addiction treatment unit if she self-identifies as a person struggling with addiction upon her arrival in the correctional facility. Women who have previously been arrested on prostitution charges and tested positive for HIV upon completion of a court-mandated health order at Denver Health, the city's largest hospital, can face felony charges that will send them to prison if convicted.

At the hearing, the judge could also recommend a woman for participation in a problem-solving court, typically referred to as "diversion court" because of its intended purpose to support women in redirecting their lives away from illicit drug use and prostitution. These courts require participants to appear weekly before the judge to report on their progress toward the goals of sobriety, obtaining stable housing and legal work, and other specialized criteria determined by the court. Probation officers, as well as therapeutic support staff, supervise participants through mandatory drug testing and additional regular meetings.

The judge could likewise permit a woman to enter a transitional housing program, where a caseworker will report positive drug tests or unapproved absences to probation, resulting in the woman's subsequent arrest and incarceration. This system is almost Byzantine in its complexity, and research conducted as part of this study endeavored whenever possible to mirror women's trajectories through the criminal justice, social services, and healthcare systems that shape their lives and often considerably restrict their autonomy.

Methodology

Ongoing for 5 years, my work in Denver comprised an iterative methodology that commenced when I received permission, in 2011, to live and work as unpaid staff at a transitional housing facility for street-involved women. I spent approximately 4 days and 3 nights per week over the course of a year engaged in participant observation with the women and staff members. As I attended addictions and other therapeutic groups, waited to apply for social service benefits, grocery shopped, and engaged in other mundane activities, the women and I created bonds characterized by all the accompanying complexities and dysfunction that the term "family" implies.

I used my spare time at the facility to enter demographic case file data into an electronic spreadsheet for use by facility staff (as well as my research), which provided valuable quantitative information on hundreds of women that balanced my qualitative participant observation and subsequent interview results. Women's self-reported ethno-racial backgrounds, in the facility as on the street, reflect the gendered socioeconomic inequalities that frame their lives more generally. While there are women of all ethno-racial backgrounds working the street, it is significant that just under half (46.5 %) of the women self-identify as White in a city where 70 % of Census respondents self-identify with this category (US Census Bureau 2012). As in other US cities, White privilege informs broader cultural-sexual norms and imposes constraints upon the abilities of women of color to pursue more lucrative forms of sex work. White women accordingly predominate in lower risk, higher income forms of sex work, such as exotic dancing and escorting.

My gradual integration into the cultural and spatial world of the street through the intimacies of shared living space allowed me to conduct 200 interviews, 100 of which I was able to record, with street-involved women in the East Colfax motels where they live and work, in the transitional housing facility, and in correctional facilities. I conducted 28 of these interviews with women as part of a collaborative project with medical anthropologist Treena Orchard in which we examined the healthcare and social service experiences of women in our respective research sites in the United States and Canada. As part of this project, I also conducted 25 interviews with healthcare and social service providers who regularly interact with the women. I received permission, in the fifth year of the research, to observe in a Denver area prostitution diversion court, which I complemented with regular observations in a county court, which is open to the public. As part of my work with the transitional housing facility, I also often attended county court as an advocate for women who had pending cases and interviewed approximately two dozen criminal justice professionals about their experiences working with the women.

My integration into the women's lives and cultural norms became so thorough that, in summer 2014, the transitional housing facility's Executive Director asked me to take on the role of intake coordinator. I made the decision to formally cease data collection a year later, when it became apparent that I had interacted with or formally interviewed a significant number of street-involved women and the professionals they regularly encounter. In this pro bono role, I am the first point of contact for women who wish to enter the program, which provides a year of housing, addictions, and therapeutic treatment. The wide reach of the US criminal justice system into the women's lives means that, for many women, entering a program that focuses on addiction treatment is their only alternative to long-term incarceration. The ability to meet and offer much-needed services to women in jail, prison, and on the street, and coordinate with the social service and criminal justice professionals tasked with managing their "cases," allows me to contribute meaningfully to the lives of women who have so generously and bravely shared their stories with me.

Concise Summary Overview of Chapters and Key Arguments

Employing the exclusionary regime as a framing mechanism, this chapter has illustrated how criminalization consistently results in conditions that further marginalize women who sell or trade sex. Subsequent chapters support this argument with evidence from our respective field sites in China, Canada, and the United States. Chapter 2, "Systematic Collusion: Criminalization's Health and Safety Consequences," argues that criminalization negatively impacts women's health and safety by systematically excluding them from healthcare and the right to earn an income without fear of violence or punitive sanctions. Chapter 3, "Negotiating Systematic Collusion: Autonomy, Citizenship, and Resistance," describes some of the strategies women who sell or trade sex develop within sociolegal systems that target them as victims, agents of contagion, and criminal perpetrators who willfully disregard the law, including arrest avoidance strategies, cultivation of support networks, and involvement in extralegal activities other than sex work. Chapter 4, "Researchers' Negotiations of Systematic Collusion," documents researchers' strategies for ethically engaging with the women in politically fraught environments associated with criminalized, stigmatized activities.

References

Abel, G., L. Fitzgerald, C. Healy, and A. Taylor. 2010. *Taking the Crime out of Sex Work: New Zealand Sex Workers' Fight for Decriminalization*. Bristol: The Policy Press.
Agustín, L. 2007. *Sex at the Margins: Migration, Labour Markets, and the Sex Industry*. London: Zed Books.
Andanda, Pamela. 2009. Vulnerability: Sex Workers in Nairobi's Majengo Slum. *Cambridge Quarterly of Healthcare Ethics* 18(2): 138–146.

Benoit, C., C. Atchison, L. Casey, M. Jansson, B. McCarthy, R. Phillips, B. Reimer, D. Reist, and F. Shaver. 2014. *A "Working Paper" Prepared as Background to "Building on the Evidence: An International Symposium on the Sex Industry in Canada."* Victoria, British Columbia, Canada.

Berger, S. 2012. No End in Sight: Why the "End Demand" Movement Is the Wrong Focus for Efforts to Eliminate Human Trafficking. *Harvard Journal of Law & Gender* 35: 523–570.

Blanchette, T., and A. da Silva. 2011. Prostitution in Contemporary Rio de Janeiro. In *Policing Pleasure: Sex Work, Policy, and the State in Global Perspective*, ed. S. Dewey and P. Kelly, 130–145. New York: New York University Press.

Brents, B., C. Jackson, and K. Hausbeck. 2009. *The State of Sex: Tourism, Sex, and Sin in the New American Heartland.* New York: Routledge.

Brewer, D., J. Dudek, J. Potterat, S. Muth, J. Roberts, and D. Woodhouse. 2006. Extent, Trends, and Perpetrators of Prostitution-Related Homicide in the United States. *Journal of Forensic Science* 51: 1101–1108.

Bruckert, C. 2002. *Taking It off, Putting It on: Women in the Strip Trade.* London: The Women's Press.

Bunch, M. 2014. Communicating for the Purposes of Human Rights: Sex Work and Discursive Justice in Canada. *Canadian Journal of Human Rights* 3(1): 39–74.

Butler, A. 1986. *Daughters of Joy, Sisters of Misery: Prostitutes in the American West, 1865-90.* Champaign: University of Illinois Press.

Cameron, S. 2010. *On the Farm: Robert William Pickton and the Tragic Story of Vancouver's Missing Women.* Toronto: Knopf.

City of London. 2011. *East London Neighbourhood Profile.* London: Policy Division-Policy Planning and Programs.

Crago, A. 2008. *Our Lives Matter: Sex Workers Unite for Health and Human Rights.* New York: Open Society Institute.

Csete, J., and J. Cohen. 2010. Health Benefits of Legal Services for Criminalized Populations: The Case of People Who Use Drugs, Sex Workers and Sexual and Gender Minorities. *Journal of Law, Medicine & Ethics* 38(4): 816–831.

Cunningham, V. 1976. *London in the Bush 1826–1976.* London, ON: London Public Library Board.

Deering, K., A. Amin, J. Shoveller, A. Nesbitt, C. Garcia-Moreno, P. Duff, E. Argento, and K. Shannon. 2014. A Systematic Review of the Correlates of Violence Against Sex Workers. *American Journal of Public Health* 104(4): E42–E45.

Denver Office of Drug Strategy. 2012. *Proceedings of the Denver Epidemiology Work Group.* http://www.denvergov.org/Portals/692/documents/DEWG%20Proceedings_July2012.pdf.

Denver Police Department. 2015. *2015 Crime Statistics & Maps.* http://www.denvergov.org/police/PoliceDepartment/CrimeInformation/CrimeStatisticsMaps/tabid/441370/Default.aspx.

Dewey, S. 2008. *Hollow Bodies: Institutional Responses to Sex Trafficking in Armenia, Bosnia, and India.* Sterling: Kumarian Press.

———. 2014. Recovery Narratives, War Stories, and Nostalgia: Street-Based Sex Workers' Discursive Negotiations of the Exclusionary Regime. *Anthropological Quarterly* 87(4): 1131–1157.

Dewey, S., and T. Zheng. 2013. *Ethical Research with Sex Workers: Anthropological Approaches.* New York: Springer Press.

Dewey, S., and T. St. Germain. 2014. Sex Workers/Sex Offenders: Exclusionary Criminal Justice Practices in New Orleans. *Feminist Criminology* 10(3): 211–234.

Dewey, S., S. Jane, for The Sex Workers' Outreach Project New Orleans, and Jenny Heineman, for the Sex Workers' Outreach Project (SWOP) Las Vegas. 2013. Between Research and Activism: Identifying Pathways to Inclusive Research. In *Ethical Research with Sex Workers: Anthropological Approaches*, ed. S. Dewey and T. Zheng, 57–96. New York: Springer.

Dodge, M., D. Starr-Gimeno, and T. Williams. 2005. Puttin' on the Sting: Women Police Officers' Perspectives on Reverse Prostitution Assignments. *International Journal of Police Science & Management* 7(2): 71–92.

References

Farley, M. 2004. Bad for the Body, Bad for the Heart: Prostitution Harms Women Even if legalized or Decriminalized. *Violence Against Women* 10(10): 1087–1125.

Ferris, S. 2015. *Street Sex Work and Canadian Cities: Resisting a Dangerous Order*. Edmonton: University of Alberta Press.

Gillespie, I. 2011. They Love Old East Village, But… *London Free Press*. http://www.lfpress.com/news/columnists/ian_gillespie/2011/11/10/18952681.html (Accessed November 11, 2011).

Leigh, C. 1997. Inventing Sex Work. In *Whores and Other Feminists*, ed. J. Nagle, 225–231. New York: Routledge.

Katsulis, Y. 2008. *Sex Work and the City: The Social Geography of Health and Safety in Tijuana, Mexico*. Austin: University of Texas Press.

Kelly, P. 2008. *Lydia's Open Door: Inside Mexico's Most Modern Brothel*. Berkeley: University of California Press.

Kerouac, J. 1957. *On the Road*. New York: Penguin.

Khruakham, S., and B. Lawton. 2012. Assessing the Impact of the 1996 Thai Prostitution Law: A Study of Police Arrest Data. *Asian Journal of Criminology* 7(1): 23–36.

Kotiswaran, P. 2014. Beyond the Allures of Criminalization: Rethinking the Regulation of Sex Work in India. *Criminology & Criminal Justice* 14(5): 565–579.

Kurtz, S., H. Surratt, M. Kiley, and J. Inciardi. 2005. Barriers to Health and Social Services for Street-Based Sex Workers. *Journal of Health Care for the Poor and Underserved* 16(2): 345–361.

Landry, A. 2013. Native history: The birth of Denver, from boom to bust to boom. *Indian Country Today*, October 29. http://indiancountrytodaymedianetwork.com/2013/10/29/native-history-when-worlds-collide-first-store-opens-denver-1858-151971.

Lawrence, S. 2015. Expert-Tease: Advocacy, Ideology, and Experience in *Bedford* and Bill C-36. *Canadian Journal of Law and Society* 39(1): 5–7.

Leonard, S., and J. Noel. 1991. *Denver: Mining Camp to Metropolis*. Boulder: University Press of Colorado.

MacKell, J. 2007. *Brothels, Bordellos, & Bad Girls: Prostitution in Colorado, 1860-1930*. Albuquerque: University of New Mexico Press.

———. 2009. *Red Light Women of the Rocky Mountains*. Albuquerque: University of New Mexico Press.

Mahdavi, P. 2010. Race, Space, Place: Notes on the Racialisation and Spatialisation of Commercial Sex Work in Dubai, UAE. *Culture, Health & Sexuality* 12(8): 943–954.

Metro Denver Economic Development Corporation. 2015. *Population*. http://www.metrodenver.org/do-business/demographics/population/.

Metro Denver Homelessness Initiative. 2014. *2014 State of Homelessness Report: Seven-County Denver Metropolitan Region*. http://mdhi.org/wp-content/uploads/2014/06/PIT-report-2014-6-17.pdf.

Miller, O. 1988. *This Was London— The First Two Centuries*, Westport, ON: Butternut Press.

"Miss Colfax". 2014. "*Miss Colfax*". http://www.colfaxavenue.com/p/miss-colfax_8.html.

Mitchell, G. 2011. Organizational Challenges Facing Male Sex Workers in Brazil's Tourist Zones. In *Policing Pleasure: Sex Work, Policy, and the State in Global Perspective*, ed. S. Dewey and P. Kelly, 159–171. New York: New York University Press.

Morris, M., B. Dahl, L. Breslin, K. Berger, A. Finger, and A. Alejano-Steele. 2012. *Prostitution and Denver's Criminal Justice System: Who Pays?* Denver, CO: Laboratory to Combat Human Trafficking. http://www.ccasa.org/wp-content/uploads/2014/01/Prostitution-and-denvers-criminal-justice-system-who-pays.pdf.

Murray, M. 2002. City Profile: Denver. *Cities* 19(4): 283–294.

Orchard, T. 2015. "So It's Always a Dance": The Politics of Gifts and Governance at a Drop-in Centre for Vulnerable Women in London, Ontario. In *Neoliberal Governance and Health: Duties, Risks, and Vulnerabilities*, eds. J. Polzer and E. Power. Montreal: McGill-Queens Press.

Orchard, T., S. Farr, S. Macphail, C. Wender, and D. Young. 2012. Sex Work in the Forest City: Sex Work Beginnings, Types, and Clientele Among Women in London, Ontario. *Sexuality Research & Social Policy* 9(4): 350–362.

_____. 2013. Resistance, Negotiation, and Management of Identity Among Women in the Sex Trade in London, Ontario. *Culture, Health & Sexuality* 15(2): 191–204.
Orchard, T., S. Farr, S. Macphail, C. Wender, and C. Wilson. 2014. Expanding the Scope of Inquiry: Exploring Accounts of Childhood and Family Among Canadian Sex Workers. *Canadian Journal of Human Sexuality* 23(1): 9–18.
Pan, S., and Y. Huang. 2011. Evaluation of the effect of 2010 massive police raids. (2010 Nian Dasaohuang Xiaoguo de Pinggu). *Rights and Multidimension: Essays from the Third International Symposium on Sexual Research in China* (Quanli Yu Duoyuan: Disanjie Xingyanjiu Guoji Yantaohui Lunwenji). Beijing: The Center for Disease Control.
Piano, D. 2011. Working the Streets of Post-Katrina New Orleans: An Interview with Deon Haywood, Executive Director, Women with a Vision, Inc. *Women's Studies Quarterly* 39(3/4): 201–218.
Quinet, K. 2011. Prostitutes as Victims of Serial Homicide: Trends and Case Characteristics, 1970-2009. *Homicide Studies* 15: 74–100.
Richter, M. 2013. Characteristics, Sexual Behavior and Access to Healthcare for Sex Workers in South Africa. *Afrika Focus* 26(2): 165–176.
Salfati, C., A. James, and L. Ferguson. 2008. Prostitute Homicides: A Descriptive Study. *Journal of Interpersonal Violence* 23(4): 505–543.
Sanders, T., and R. Campbell. 2014. Criminalization, Protection and Rights: Global Tensions in the Governance of Commercial Sex. *Criminology & Criminal Justice* 14(5): 535–548.
Shannon, K., T. Kerr, S. Allinott, J. Chettiar, J. Shoveller, and M. Tyndall. 2008. Social and Structural Violence and Power Relations in Mitigating HIV Risk of Drug-Using Women in Survival Sex Work. *Social Science & Medicine* 66(4): 911–921.
Simić, Milena, and Tim Rhodes. 2009. Violence, Dignity and HIV Vulnerability: Street Sex Work in Serbia. *Sociology of Health & Illness* 31(1): 1–16.
Statistics Canada. 2006. *City of London-Community Profile of Population and Housing, Age and Sex, Ethno-cultural Diversity, and Relationship Status and Family Characteristics*. Ottawa, ON: Statistics Canada.
Statistics Canada. 2010/2011. Average Counts of Adults in Correctional Services, by Jurisdiction. http://www.statcan.gc.ca/pub/85-002x/2012001/article/11715/tbl/tbl03-eng.htm.
Tucker, J., H. Peng, K. Wang, H. Chang, S. Zhang, L. Yang, and B. Yang. 2011. Female Sex Worker Social Networks and STI/HIV Prevention in South China. *PLoS One* 6(9): 1–6.
US Census Bureau. 2012. State and County Quickfacts: Denver. Washington, DC: US Census Bureau. http://quickfacts.census.gov/qfd/states/41/4159000.html.
Wahab, S., and M. Panichelli. 2013. Ethical and Human Rights Issues in Coercive Interventions with Sex Workers. *Affilia: Journal of Women and Social Work* 28(4): 344–349.
Walmsley, R. 2013. *World Prison Population List*, 10th ed. London: International Centre for Prison Studies.
Weitzer, R. 2011. *Legalizing Prostitution: From Illicit Vice to Lawful Business*. New York: New York University Press.
World Health Organization, UNFPA, UNAIDS, NSWP, and World Bank. 2013. *Implementing Comprehensive HIV/STI Programmes with Sex Workers: Practical Approaches from Collaborative Interventions*. Ch 2, "Addressing Violence Against Sex Workers". http://www.who.int/hiv/pub/sti/sex_worker_implementation/swit_chpt2.pdf.
Wyckoff, W. 1992. Denver's Aging Commercial Strip. *Geographical Review* 82(3): 282–294.
Zheng, T. 2009a. *Red Lights: The Lives of Sex Workers in Postsocialist China*. Minneapolis: University of Minnesota Press.
_____. 2009b. *Ethnographies of Prostitution in Contemporary China: Gender Relations, HIV/AIDS, and Nationalism*. New York: Palgrave Macmillan Press.
Zheng, T. 2010. Complexity of Female Sex Workers' Collective Actions in Postsocialist China. *Wagadu, A Journal of Transnational Women's and Gender Studies* 8: 34–70.

Chapter 2
Systematic Collusion: Criminalization's Health and Safety Consequences

The Impact of Sex Work's Legal Status on Health and Safety

National and municipal legislation, the presence or absence of active sex workers' rights movements, and international legal and rights frameworks all impact the health of women involved in the sex industry (Overs and Hawkins 2011). Chapter 1 argued that criminalization negatively impacts women who trade sex by forcing them to work in isolated and potentially dangerous locations and fostering mistrust of authority figures, both of which severely limit their abilities to find legal work and housing, and the possibility of collective rights-based organizing. This section provides an alternative to these disturbing realities in its discussion of international research that documents the improved access to healthcare and other protections sex workers enjoy in countries or locales that have decriminalized or legalized the exchange of sex for money between consenting adults. Analysis presented here focuses primarily upon the ways in which legal frameworks impact the women's access to healthcare, relations with the criminal justice system, and interactions with clients.

Harm reduction advocates and human rights organizations almost universally support the decriminalization of prostitution because of the positive associations between decriminalization and increased access to healthcare and safer working environments among sex workers (Rekart 2005; UNAIDS 2012). A comparative study in three Australian cities with different regulatory frameworks found that while the legal status of prostitution did not impact the size of the sex industry, the decriminalization of sex work in Sydney resulted in increased peer-to-peer support and health promotion activities among women not seen in Melbourne or Perth, where prostitution is still subject to criminalization (Harcourt et al. 2010). It is important to note that women who work in decriminalized contexts may still face stigma when seeking healthcare due to the unfortunate fact that no state or municipality can effectively enforce fair and equitable stigma-free treatment, which must come from systemic social change rather than the blunt force of the law. Nonetheless, compared to those working in criminalized contexts, women under decriminalization report fewer instances of delaying or abstaining from seeking healthcare services due to stigmatizing treatment or fear of incurring punitive sanctions (Overs and Loff 2013).

Research indicates that barriers to seeking and obtaining healthcare can be overcome even in criminalized contexts, as is evident in Calcutta's Sonagachi Project, which focused primarily on HIV/STI prevention as well as collectivization of women's rights. The organizers of this project attribute its success to their framing of HIV and STIs as occupational health problems and not stigmatized sexual issues confined to morally corrupt or medically dangerous women, as they traditionally had been in India. They approached their health promotion and collectivization work by involving sex workers in condom distribution, improving communication about health and disease between the women themselves and their clients, and increasing the involvement of women in sex work in community life (Smarajit et al. 2004). The model of sex worker collectivization developed in Sonagachi has also been successfully implemented in Brazil's decriminalized context, where it enabled women to insist upon client condom use as well as to participate more fully in community organizations outside the sex industry, thereby increasing their occupational safety while decreasing social isolation (Kerrigan et al. 2008).

The decriminalization of sex work and the attendant recognition of the rights of women in sex work have also been shown to decrease the burden of HIV in Australia. Sex workers' rights advocates and public health researchers contend that the country's relatively low incidence of HIV is due, in large part, to government support for different pro-sex work agencies and health promotion programming designed specifically for these women (Bates and Berg 2014). Findings from the state of New South Wales, which decriminalized sex work in 1995, indicate 99 % condom use among sex workers and historically low rates of sexually transmitted infections. These successes are attributed largely to the partnerships developed between sex workers and the New South Wales Department of Public Health (Donovan et al. 2010) as well as the recognition of sex workers as sex educators. Doing so recognizes the important communication that takes place in transactional sexual exchanges as well as the emotional labor that sex industry workers provide to their clients, which many describe as of equal or even greater importance than the sexual services purchased (Bernstein 2007; Frank 2002; Sanders 2005).

In contrast to these positive examples of increased health and safety under decriminalization the criminalization framework creates adversarial relationships between women and various officials who exert considerable control over their lives, including those in criminal justice. These conditions make it very difficult for women to report crimes against them or to hold officers accountable for their abuse of power, which is a serious issue in many settings. For instance, researchers working on a Soros Foundation-funded participatory project led by the Sex Workers' Rights Advocacy Network, a conglomeration of 16 non-governmental organizations working in 15 countries throughout Eastern and Central Europe and Central Asia, concluded that "human rights abuses committed by police against sex workers in the countries studied… cannot be dismissed as simply the acts of rogue officers, but are rightly considered manifestations of state policies that tolerate, and in some cases even encourage, violence against sex workers" (Crago 2009, p. 17). Another participatory study, conducted with the Cambodian Prostitutes' Union, surveyed 1000 women and transgender people who sell sex and found that in the past year half had been beaten by police and a third had been gang-raped by police (Jenkins et al. 2006). Likewise, interviews conducted by peer outreach workers who engage with female, male, and transgender sex workers in Kenya, South Africa, Uganda, and Zimbabwe indicated that police confiscate condoms as evidence, physically or sexually abuse sex workers, and sometimes detain them without charges (Scorgie et al. 2013).

Research indicates that police confiscation of condoms as evidence of the intent to engage in prostitution occurs in almost all areas that criminalize prostitution, further compromising women's health and safety and their mistrust of police. A project that explored this issue in South Africa, Zimbabwe, Russia, Namibia, the United States, and Kenya found that between half and 80 % of sex workers had been harassed by police, had condoms confiscated by police, or decided not to carry condoms due to their concerns about police harassment (Shields 2012). In another study with 200 sex workers and 110 outreach workers in 4 US cities, researchers found that police often used condoms as evidence of the intent to engage in prostitution (Wurth et al. 2013). Legalizing or decriminalizing prostitution places police and women who sell sex in a neutral or even positive relationship, wherein the women have the same rights to report crimes against them or others as their peers in less stigmatized occupations. Police in Victoria, Australia, for instance, can refer to a best practices guide entitled "Interacting with Sex Workers" that advises them about respectful ways of professionally relating to women who sell or trade sex (Office of Police Integrity 2008).

The interactions between women in sex work and their male clients are diverse and while they are not universally violent or dangerous, the criminalization of prostitution has been demonstrated to negatively affect these encounters (Jeffrey and MacDonald 2006). Under criminalization women are often less able to negotiate condom use or the terms of the sexual transaction with clients in settings when they fear arrest, police harassment, or assaults from their clients who are also anxious about arrest (Blankenship and Koester 2002; Shannon and Csete 2010). The ability of sex workers to organize and teach each other about techniques for screening clients and protecting themselves is also significantly reduced in criminalized settings (Redwood 2013). Some clients harbor misogynistic ideas about women in sex work and these dangerous beliefs can be exacerbated when sex work is criminalized, given the tendency for the criminal justice system to not take incidents of violence against sex workers seriously. This was tragically illustrated in the case of Robert Pickton in Coquitlam, British Columbia, who admitted to killing 49 sex workers in Vancouver's Downtown Eastside in the late 1990s-early 2000s. He expressed chilling impunity when explaining that he murdered these women not only because he hated them, but because no one would miss them (Cameron 2010).

As the following three case studies from China, Canada, and the United States demonstrate, the criminalization of prostitution severely compromises the health and safety of women who sell or trade sex.

Case Study One: China

Systematic collusion not only stigmatizes and marginalizes sex workers, but also leads to a violent, exploitative working environment, hostesses' disaffiliation with their group, and risks that have a deleterious impact on their health and safety.

A Violent Working Environment

China's crimination of sex work has resulted in a violent working environment that threatens the safety and health of sex workers, rather than eliminating sex work. Due to sex work's illegality, hostesses find it impossible to report to the police the violence they have received from the police, clients, and gangsters. Hostesses arrested at the time of my research had to endure physical abuse from the police, who often slapped their faces, kicked their stomachs, and severely beat their bodies. During the 2010 large-scale police raids, many sex workers were photographed and paraded barefoot on the street for the public to watch and humiliate (Xie 2010). In this climate of fear, hostesses have no alternative but to offer police officers sexual services without payment when requested, and bar owners admonish the hostesses to submit to police officials' sexual demands and offer free sexual services. Police clients often threaten hostesses that they will arrest the women and bring a platoon of officers to raid their bars if the hostesses are not obedient to their sexual demands.

Such forces render hostesses legally and socially vulnerable to robbery, blackmail, rape, and murder. During my research, police who discovered the bodies of murdered hostesses found it impossible to identify them due to hostesses' self-protective use of pseudonyms and fabricated places of origin to protect themselves from client stalking. For instance, hostess Wu's mother told me that when she had not heard from Wu for a while, she thought that one of Wu's clients had surely murdered her in the city. Hostesses' illegal status not only increased their risk of violent death but also subjected them to robbery, blackmail, and physical abuse, in which case, hostesses had no choice but to comply and endure. They were ever cognizant of the fact that they would be subject to extreme humiliation, arrest, fines, and incarceration if a client disclosed about their transactional sexual services to the police. For instance, during a sexual encounter in a hotel room, one of hostess Mei's clients inserted a tightly folded 100 yuan note into her vagina, its sharp edges causing a hemorrhage that soaked the bedsheet in blood when they unfurled. The client left her paralyzed by pain, and it took her months and a series of surgeries to finally recover. In such situations, hostesses suffered both physical harm and financial loss without legal recourse or the ability to report such instances to police.

Clients, well aware of hostesses' criminalized and vulnerable status, also abused hostesses inside karaoke bars. Hostesses' services for karaoke bar clients often ranged from 1 to 4 hours, during which time they needed to satisfy their clients through dancing, conversing, and drinking with them. If a client was not pleased with a hostess's service, he could replace her with someone else in the middle of her service. In such case, despite the fact this hostess had been serving him for several hours, she had no choice but to leave without compensation. To please clients, hostesses would often comply with clients' desires, including physical abuse. In the bars, clients, at times, threw beer bottles and glass at hostesses or pinched hostesses' legs, arms, and breasts black and blue. Hostesses often came downstairs, crying from their injuries from clients. Some hostesses clenched their teeth to endure the abuse for the final payment, whereas others quit in the middle and ultimately received no payment for their time.

Hostesses' illegal and vulnerable status also enabled bar bouncers to abuse hostesses who were not submissive to their orders. In Romantic Dreams, for instance, when other bar owners came to borrow hostesses to serve in their bars, the bar bouncer picked out some hostesses to help out with the other bar owners. At times when some hostesses refused to go, he shut them in a room and beat them up. Other times, hostesses at Romantic Dreams were unsatisfied with the slow business and contemplated leaving the bar to work somewhere else. The bar bouncer warned everyone that since he knew all bar owners in the karaoke bar circle throughout the city, he would learn about their presence in other bars. He claimed that he would beat them to death if they dared to escape to other bars to work without his knowledge. Some hostesses did slip away from Romantic Dreams to work in other bars, but upon their return the bar bouncer beat them severely and warned other hostesses that they would receive the same treatment if they failed to obey his orders.

Madams, too, used violence to discipline the hostesses. In the upscale bar, for instance, when I was sitting in the dressing room, a hostess rushed in, telling me that her client had been pinching her legs so she needed to change into pants to hide the bruises. While she was changing, the furious madam came in, slapped the hostess's face, hit her in the head with her big interphone, and bellowed, "Don't you know that your client is looking for you? Why are you hiding here? I have been looking for you everywhere! I am ordering you to go back to your client immediately!" The hostess tried to dodge the madam's blows as her face reddened from the madam's slaps. She responded quickly to reassure the madam, "Sure, sure, I will go back right away." Fleeing the madam's violence and harsh words, she quickly slipped out of the room.

In addition to the police, clients, bar bouncer, and madams, gangsters also came into the bar at unexpected times to bully hostesses. They pulled attractive hostesses to the sex room upstairs and raped them, slapping and beating hostesses they did not sexually desire. Most of the bar hostesses had been raped once or more times by gangsters, who terrified them. As soon as they saw the gangsters entering the door, they would exert all their efforts to escape. On one occasion we fled together, climbing over the back wall all the way up to the railroad on the top of the bar. Although we cut our feet and lost our shoes, the narrow escape was something to celebrate afterwards.

All bars I worked in hired a talented street fighter as a bar bouncer to maintain security and ensure client payment; without such a person, itinerant gangsters would harass and plunder the bar. During my research at Romantic Dreams, I saw numerous bloody fights between the bar bouncer and gangsters, clients, and passersby, who threw heavy rocks, chairs, and beer bottles at each other's heads and faces. The bar owner told me that if his bar bouncer did not enjoy such a fierce reputation as a man convicted of killing several men, the bar would have to close down because hostesses would run away in fear and the bar would be robbed by gangsters.

An Exploitative Environment

My research revealed that police crackdowns in the mid-1990s had terminated the contract system between hostesses and bar owners and ushered in an exploitative system that continues today. Prior to the police crackdowns, hostesses were hired on contracts by bar owners. These contracts guaranteed hostesses a percentage of customers' bills of drinks, snacks, and room rentals, as well as fees from customers for hostesses' services. This contract system was brought to an end in the mid-1990s when an extreme police crackdown disrupted the previous system and ended the percentage award to hostesses by bar owners. The crackdown resulted from an incident wherein a foreigner was chased out of the red light district in his underwear, by Chinese men with clubs in their hands, for failing to pay for his previous night's sexual encounter. This foreigner eventually brought charges against the bar's proprietor for exploiting him, quickly escalating this local incident into an international conflict between the two affected embassies and prompting the Communist Central Committee to immediately order sweeping police raids in the area.

Ever since this incident, local government has exercised strict control over bar hostesses and owners, causing bar owners to perceive themselves as saviors of the hostesses who work for them. From then on, owners terminated the percentage award to hostesses and started requiring hostesses to turn in 10 % of their fees to them. Bar owners also set a minimal consumption level for each client, a responsibility falling on the shoulder of hostesses. While serving the clients, hostesses were obligated to order and consume a huge amount of alcohol to make the bill reach the consumption level. The bathroom was filled with suffocating smells of alcohol and food that hostesses vomited into the toilet. In Romantic Dreams, clients were normally required to give a 100-yuan tip (US$16) to hostesses, out of which 10 yuan (US$1.6) should be submitted to the owner as the stage fee. This stage fee could be waived if the hostesses were able to bring in 240 *yuan* (US$38) worth of consumption from their clients in the karaoke room. Hostess Dee said to me,

> Once I was sitting with two other hostesses in the karaoke room. We agreed among ourselves to drink twenty-four big bottles of beer (10 *yuan* per large bottle, totaling 240 yuan) to have the stage fee waived. So we started drinking crazily to death. We almost gave up our whole lives for it. We went to the bathroom to vomit. When we could not throw up any longer, we used our fingers to help. We did not care about the severe stomachache but came back to the room and started drinking again. At last, only one bottle was left, but none of us could finish it. Just because of this one bottle, the managers refused to waive the stage fee.

Hostesses were required to pay the bar owners both the onstage fee and offstage (sex work) fee. In the low-tier bar, the price of sexual service was negotiated between clients and bar owners, without the knowledge of hostesses. Hostesses' payment was set at 200–300 yuan (US$32–48) per sexual service, and 400 yuan (US$64) for a whole night's sexual services. The price for a whole night was much higher than 1 or 2 hours of sexual services, in which case the bar owner kept as much as half of the clients' payment.

During my research in the upscale karaoke bar, the bar owner capitalized on hostesses' fear of constant police raids to enforce new demands, controls, and restrictions on hostesses. For instance, the owner required hostesses to arrive at the bar at 7:30 p.m. every day and not leave until 12 a.m. unless they went out with clients for sexual services, in which case they had to report to the bar owner and submit the appropriate stage fees. Hostesses who came late or left early were fined 600 yuan (US$97), and owners rarely granted hostesses' request for a leave or a night off. Hence intensified enforcement of criminalization allowed the bar owner to further exploit hostesses and ensure the prosperity of the bar business.

Group Disaffiliation

Criminalization results in the hostesses' stigmatization and marginalization, which pushes many hostesses to disaffiliate with the group through aspirations to move up the social ladder. This motivation drove them to pursue individual economic interests without consideration of other hostesses' welfare. The high frequency of police raids over extended periods often led to economic deprivation as hostesses regularly had to stop work in order to hide from police. Once arrested, hostesses had to submit substantial fines that resulted in further financial pressures and consequent intense internal competition, as did the knowledge that "spy hostesses" worked as police informants. These factors combined with hostesses' use of pseudonyms and fabricated identities to make hostesses extremely cautious in their interactions with each other.

Hostesses' intense competition for clients often led them to "steal" each other's regular clients or avoid introducing such men to their colleagues. For instance, hostesses Hong and Liu were close friends, but Hong never introduced her boyfriend to Liu. One day Hong asked Liu to help her move into her boyfriend's apartment at 8 a.m. Sunday morning, telling Liu that her boyfriend would be there. Liu arrived at 8 a.m., but did not see her boyfriend, and after completing the move, Hong asked Liu to leave as her boyfriend would be returning. In fact, Hong had arranged her boyfriend to arrive at 9:30 a.m. so that Liu could never meet him. Hong's caution was sensible as it was common for hostesses to snatch each other's clients and boyfriends. In this as well as many other examples, the transient nature of hostesses' small informal networks stems from their aspirations to defect from the criminalized hostess group and its intense internal competition.

Health Risks

The use of condoms as evidence of sex work during police raids and police harassment impedes hostesses' condom use with clients and increases the hostesses' likelihood of acquiring sexually transmitted infections. Such continued use of condoms as evidence to arrest hostesses as sex workers directly violates the current laws, including the 2006 Law on AIDS Prevention (Wen 2006) which clearly stipulates that the police should not use condoms as evidence and that condoms should be made accessible by business proprietors at public places. The State Council 2012 Proposal (Office of State Council 2012) further stipulates that condoms should be made available at public places and that proprietors should strive to promote their use.

During my research, when the hostesses were arrested, they were subjected to a body search for the presence of condoms and used them as evidence to charge the hostesses for engaging in prostitution. In the most recent 2010 nationwide crackdown on sex work, condoms continued to be employed as the proof for charges of sex work (Pan and Huang 2011). Fear of police arrest and detention based on the evidence of condoms discouraged hostesses from protecting themselves with safe sex. The practice of unsafe sex compromised hostesses' health by exposing them to infections.

Some hostesses chose to continue to work during the police raids, albeit in more clandestine locations and in different forms. While normally hostesses engaged in sex work in the sex room on the second floor in Romantic Dreams, during police raids, they had no choice but to follow clients to their places. Help was beyond reach in those strange, unfamiliar places such as rented apartments that were far away from the neighborhood of the bars. Hostesses were much more vulnerable to clients' use of violence and practice of unsafe sex, harming their health and enhancing the possibilities for infections. Other hostesses fled the police raids by moving back to their rural hometowns for several months, and the resulting economic deprivation and financial loss precipitated an intense internal competition and an incentive to engage in unsafe sex to earn more money when they eventually resumed work.

As I have explored elsewhere (Zheng 2009b), hostesses adopted various methods to ward off potential sexually transmitted infections, such as taking emergency contraceptive pills, relying on ineffective liquid condoms and external-use cleansing liquids, using their judgment, and getting pre-sex antibiotic injections on the advice of medical professionals who insist these can cure any diseases contracted. These practices, such as overdose of contraceptive pills and overuse of cleansing liquids and antibiotic shots, not only were ineffective in preventing sexually transmitted infections but also resulted in infertility, heavy vomiting, irregular periods, severe abdominal pain, and frequent pregnancies and abortions; during my research, almost every hostess had undergone between one and ten abortions.

During my research at hospitals that treat sexually transmitted infections, doctors told me that police required them to submit the names and other information of patients who had sexually transmitted infections. This was one of the ways through which the police were able to locate and arrest hostesses, who usually avoided these high-cost hospitals and sought healthcare from low quality, low-priced, unlicensed clinics, run by unqualified practitioners without any formal medical training. Occasionally when they needed serious surgeries or their regular clients had personal networks with certain doctors, they would go to hospitals for treatment. Most often they visited these unlicensed, cheap clinics, where quack doctors would offer fast, temporary symptom relief through antibiotic shots, often at the expense of hostesses' long-term suffering.

Hostesses spent less money on basic healthcare than on body-altering drugs and cosmetic surgeries such as eyelid operations, breast augmentation, rhinoplasty, change of face shape, and eyebrow and eyeliner tattoos, all of which increased their earnings and bolstered their self-image as full-fledged urban citizens (Zheng 2009a). These consumption practices not only drained their financial resources but also resulted in their inability to receive expensive, long-term regular treatments for health problems. Juggling both health risks and financial risks, hostesses often chose to sacrifice their health for financial gains that would economically sustain their families and themselves.

Case Study Two: Canada

> They're judging you because you're one, you're a junkie. And you're on the street so they think you're dirty and full of disease…you're like the plague to them…meanwhile they don't know the circumstances…I, I have a clean, free body (Lynn).

The women in our study experience multiple physical and mental health conditions,[1] some of which are connected to their abusive and often troubled upbringings (Orchard et al. 2014) and others are linked with their current struggles with drug addiction, homelessness, and sex work participation. Addressing their health-related issues requires them to engage with endless forms of systemic administration and medical surveillance as well as the professionals working in these domains, who can be less than empathetic regarding the experiences these women have gone through and continue to face. While these forces of systematic collusion intersect in our participants' lives in unique ways, their effects on women's health and safety are often negative and harmful. However, during the interviews the women did not focus extensively on their challenges with the punitive, maze-like systems they are put through to access health or social services. What they emphasized

---

[1] Which include but are not limited to: addictions; Hepatitis C; endocarditis; abscesses; posttraumatic stress disorder; depression; anxiety; reproductive health issues; violent or abusive relationships; homelessness; HIV/AIDS; diabetes; and harassment from police, clients, and others in the East of Adelaide neighborhood. While a few women experience one or two of these issues together, the majority of our participants struggle with virtually every one of these health and safety-related challenges.

was how the stigma related to their identities as drug users and women in sex work impacted them, which is captured in Lynn's opening interview excerpt. These different yet intimately connected forms of discrimination put the women's health at risk and often reinforce their conflicted feelings of self-worth and mistrust of the systems that are ostensibly set up to help them.

The Impact of Drug User Identity on Health

When discussing the relationship between drug use and health, the women identified how individual behaviors and broader conditions informed their drug-using practices and led to many of their health issues. However, they also talked about the powerful role of drugs in the mediation of their past and present traumas, revealing the complicated place drugs occupy within the women's lived experiences: they can hurt and heal, for a time. While participants spoke at length about what led to their addictions, namely family conflict and personal tragedies and a lack of supportive networks to cope with these events, in the healthcare system these contributing factors were often ignored and they were reduced to "just" drug users. The women discussed being repeatedly assessed as "junkies" in medical settings, primarily hospitals and emergency rooms, and receiving poor healthcare, if any, on account of the degraded connotations associated with this socially stigmatized identity.

It's Your Fault

The dominant message they received from healthcare providers when they tried to address various health conditions, not only those related to their drug use, was that they were less deserving of care because they are addicts. As Melanie said: "I think the unfair assumption is that you're allowed to treat drug addicts like crap, just because they're drug addicts." Jo told us that doctors have said to her, "It's your own fault" and Patty indicated that the health professionals often get frustrated when she came for help: "It's like, another addict." Kerri recently underwent an excruciating procedure for the removal of an abscess and her experience is a particularly troubling example of the dehumanizing treatment these women receive in hospital environments on account of their "junkie" identity:

> The doctor goes, 'well you did it to yourself and now you come to me to fix you'... They wouldn't give me any painkillers, they wouldn't even freeze it. They sliced me open and they dug and dug and dug...And I couldn't handle it, was telling them to stop. They're again, like, 'you did it to yourself.'

These discriminatory practices lead many women to internalize the shame they already feel with respect to their drug use, which can sometimes fuel more intense periods of drug use or nihilistic self-harming behaviors. These experiences also result in women avoiding health services of any kind or waiting until they are in crisis or near death to go to hospitals, which exacerbates their condition.

The Problems with Methadone

Methadone maintenance programs (MMTs) are another powerful example of how the women's drug use is employed to regulate, assess, and often punish them in relation to biomedical models of health and institutionalized compliance. Prescribed in Canada and the United States since the early 1970s, methadone is a synthetic opiate that blocks the effects of opiates to help the user beat this particular drug dependency (Fischer et al. 2005; Rosenbaum 1981). One participant described what it feels like being on methadone in the following way: "It doesn't make me high and happy but it does kind of just keep the restlessness kind of at bay, a little bit" (Melanie). While it keeps opiate urges at bay for some women MMT did not enable any of our participants, all of whom were on or had been on methadone, to beat their opiate addiction. Several women expressed frustration with this form of state-sanctioned addiction, which produces very few if any positive benefits and is part of larger observable processes that rely upon the suffering of people with addictions for commercial gain and pharmaceutical dominance within particular markets. It is little wonder that women like Vicky, who has family members who have been on methadone for *decades* to no avail, question and resist the way that MMT structures people's lives: "They don't do what they're supposed to do, like put me on methadone...and then wean me off of it. I don't wanna be on methadone all my fucking life."

Several women lamented the negative health effects and the dependence engendered from being on methadone, which is taken orally in the form of a drink once a day at an assigned pharmacy/clinic or at home from a weekly supply in rare cases (i.e., carries). Janice exclaimed, "It's eating all my fucking teeth" and Vicky said: "You get sick from it, but umm basically that's how it goes. You're stuck on it." Melanie discussed feeling trapped, "If I want to move back to [another city], do they have a dispensary? I can't just up and leave this place or I'll get very sick.[2]" Another related issue brought up often in interviews is how MMT adherence is intertwined with other modes of service eligibility and dispensation, which is assessed through various forms of bodily surveillance—especially the "pee test." A "dirty pee" can be due to the ingestion of banned opiates but also the intake of prescribed psychotropic medications, both of which carry a "guilty" verdict and the loss of various vital services connected with the MMT regime (i.e., welfare, disability services, access to children, bus pass). As Mandy said: "I need to get my methadone every day. So I have to get my doctor to fill out forms saying that I'm on methadone, and then [I] get the bus pass." Women can regain their access to the program if they start from zero and conform to the behavioral and bodily surveillance upon which MMT depends, which Janice (referring specifically to carries) spoke about in terms of points that need to be earned back over time: "You gotta earn them all back, which will take another couple months."

---

[2] The withdrawal symptoms from methadone are described as being agonizing and worse than those associated with heroin or other drugs. As Vicky said, "Methadone's the worst thing to come off of. Yea, like you get seizures from it, you know, you can die from it, especially if you're at a high risk."

There are additional reasons to question the widespread prescription of methadone, namely the shifts in local drug use from primarily opioids to stimulants—particularly crystal meth. This shift is linked with provincial drug policy changes that saw the removal of opiates like *OxyContin* from the markets in 2012, due to overprescription, catastrophic levels of addiction, and death among users.[3] Crystal meth has now entered the drug scene and the lives of many women in our study with devastating effects given its psychotic-inducing behaviors and high risk of overdose. The number of overdoses linked with the drug reached 251 between January and May of this year alone, which is more than a threefold increase over the same period 2 years ago (O'Brien 2015). This example illustrates the harmful outcomes of drug policy changes that not only ignore the shifting realities of drug use in the local street scene, but keeps the women locked into ineffective "treatment" procedures that do little more than ensure their systemic dependence.

The Impact of Sex Worker Identity on Safety

Our participants have worked in strip bars, massage parlors, and other kinds of indoor contexts (i.e., escorting, chat lines); however, most were currently engaged in street-based sex work and these experiences dominated their discussions. The women's reflections on issues of personal safety, as well as those of others in the trade, focused on the legal status of sex work and the police who regulate the laws as well as many other aspects of their lives. These twin forces collide in their lives in frustrating and oppressive ways and reveal much about the culture of everyday violence (Scheper-Hughes 1992) and how it is mediated by intersecting forces of power, corruption, and the stigma associated with being identified as a "sex worker."

Laws and Safety

Our participants identified street-based work as the most dangerous kind of work they have undertaken because of police presence, the lack of appropriate time to screen clients, violence from clients, and the vulnerability associated with being visible. As Patty shared: "In a car you don't have time to beat around the bush but when working on Craigslist I was able to say, 'we're-you're spending time with me…you know, basically you're paying for my time not for what we do as adults." Their perspectives on the legal status of sex work varied, from supporting legalization and decriminalization to leaving the laws as they are. Despite their particular position they all spoke about the need for women have the choice or right to move indoors to increase their safety, as Jo said, "I think that's what they should have here is brothels. Yeah. If girls wanna go work there they can." Vicky echoed this and noted the impossibility of 'abolishing' sex work:

---

[3] Which increased by a staggering 242 % between 1991 and 2010 (Gomes et al. 2014).

> Prostitution has been here since like-like since the beginning of time and you know…it's not going anywhere so why not legalize it and put them in safe houses, like you got massage parlors and strip joints you know…just legalize everything and make it safe.

Patty advocates for decriminalization and added some interesting insights into the money and control to be gained by the government if sex work was legalized, "Decriminalization of it is good, 'cause if you legalize it then everybody wants to be a pimp, including the government."

Very few women knew about the new sex work legislation, which can be applied to indoor work, includes advertising for sexual services (which many of them do) and focuses on criminalizing those who purchase sex; the so-called Nordic or Swedish model. When asked about this particular model they indicated that it was ludicrous: "How would that stop? [laughs]. That's confusing and strange. It's their decision. We're both adults" (Jo). Denise also indicated that such a policy was futile, "They can't do that. I don't know, johns will just keep coming. They're not gonna stop, it's sex. They're gonna pay for it no matter whether they like it or not." Marnie highlighted additional problems associated with this model, namely the increased power it would give already powerful—and sometimes corrupt—members of the police force:

> So it's going to be basically up to the officer, which isn't right. It should be cut and dry, black and white, right…I'm not agreeing with that. I think they're giving way too much power to the cop and I'm telling you, I don't know too many good cops. They're crooked as hell those guys.

The Police

Many participants discussed the complex relationships they have with the police who, as they readily admit, have a job to do with respect to enforcing the laws related to sex work, drugs, violence, and various criminal activities. Several women have been given a break from the police, often when they first start working, which for some is connected with the perceptions of women in sex work as victims: "Some cops are pretty good with us because they look at us as more or less the victim…and they're more pissed off at the pimps and the drug dealers that are supplying us and make us have to be out there" (Stephanie). However, it was far more common for our participants to have negative and coercive interactions with police. For Laura, that was her rationale for doing the interview: "Because I wanted to tell you about the fuckin' cops, to be honest with you."

The women discussed multiple kinds of police exploitation, including the request for "freebies" or free sexual services in exchange for not charging them and/or "helping" them prepare for upcoming jail terms. Kerrie explained the approach taken by one well-known police officer: "He lets girls give him blowjobs and says, 'I'll give you time to get a package together'…like, dope or tobacco or whatever so you don't get dope sick in there." The ways that the police hide behind their powerful positions while taking part in criminal behavior themselves was also mentioned by several participants, including Judy who has taken part in these activities with certain police officers:

> They think they can hide behind their badge and their better. No I'm sorry you, you guys are some of the worst criminals. Where do you think the money goes when the money gets confiscated? Where do you think the dope that they pulled out of your pocket is going? Home to their house to enjoy. I know that 'cause I used to party with some.

Another strategy employed by the police is extortion and many women have been offered money from officers, often considerable amounts,[4] to provide them with information about various criminal activities taking place in the city. These offers are often made in exchange for "looking the other way" when the women are working, which participants like Lynn find offensive given that the police have done little to help her: "You don't do anything to help me!...Maybe unless I rat out a couple people for you, or become an informant!" With humor and force, Sylvia described how she responded to a police officer's recent offer of 1000 dollars to help him locate some guns connected to a local drug dealer: "'If you get me the guns I'll give you a thousand dollars'. I'm not a rat, ok. If you want the guns out this drug dealer's house, you get 'em yourself!!" The fact that these women, who struggle with not only addictions but also poverty and on-going criminalization by the police, typically refuse these propositions says a great deal about the importance of aligning with the internal power structures that run the streets versus being known as an informant or rat.

Case Study Three: The United States

Systematic collusion operates to compromise street-involved women's health and safety by restricting their abilities to seek out police assistance, disrupting peer solidarity, limiting information sharing with providers and peers, and primarily confining health diagnoses to crisis contexts that also monitor and criminalize women's HIV status. These compromising factors stem from both the criminalization of street-based prostitution and addiction as well as neighborhood contexts characterized by the illicit drug trade, gang violence, and socioeconomic deprivation.[5] Hence the primary factors that impact street-involved women's health and safety stem from the conditions in which criminalization forces them to conduct their income-generating activities, rather than from sex trading itself.

---

[4] A starting rate of 100 dollars was mentioned by several participants.
[5] The Denver Police Department's crime statistics maps classify particular areas as "high crime density," determined through a combination of calls to police and arrests made; these areas consistently include the neighborhoods where women engage in street-based prostitution (Denver Police Department 2015).

Restricted Police Aid and Reporting

Women's doubly criminalized status, due to their involvement in street-based sex work and struggles with drug addiction, restricts their ability to enlist police aid or report crimes against them. Street-involved women, most of whom are homeless or precariously housed, are targets for robbery, assault, and predatory men who seek out women who appear intoxicated or otherwise vulnerable. As 36-year-old African-American Brenda put it, "you don't wanna be lookin' homeless when you are homeless, 'cause there's guys out there out to hurt women." Women with outstanding arrest warrants, probation terms that include area restrictions forbidding them from returning to the neighborhood of their arrest, or who strongly believe that police operate with impunity, are all especially unlikely to enlist police aid. Misty, a 24-year-old White woman, concisely stated that experience with arrest and subsequent hospitalization led her to "know better" than to engage with police officers if she could avoid it:

> They kept me handcuffed...to a fuckin' bed. I had to hold for three, four hours like this, chained to a bed. And that thing around my neck was so tight it left choke marks around my neck. They had put it around my neck so tight it cut off my breathing. They didn't even put me in a room! They pushed me around the corner and left me sitting there for four hours... And then I sat there in booking for eight hours, in my own piss. And then finally, when I go to see the fucking judge, right before, they change me into fuckin' jail clothes. And then they leave me in the jail clothes for five days.

Sixty-year-old Italian-American Anita, who has worked the streets in multiple US cities since her early 20s, said that police officers had previously demanded oral sex from her in order to avoid arrest, noting, "they say, 'if you don't get back here with me we're takin' you in'." Experiences like these[6] combine with women's involvement in criminalized activities to actively dissuade them from engaging with law enforcement. Many women insisted that the police lack knowledge about serial violent offenders who target sex workers; Candy, who is 50 and White, and 29-year-old African-American Angela both described the multiple vulnerabilities that emerge from police avoidance and men who want to violently harm women:

> *Candy*: Most of them women aren't gonna turn them people in. They're just gonna tell the other girls, you know, "be leery of that person or that vehicle." I mean, you get these guys who have dungeons and they've been rapin' women and killin' women and, you know, people are found in dumpsters for a reason...there are a lot of sick-ass individuals out there.
>
> *Angela*: A girl came over the other night, she had a cast on her arm. They had to re-break three of her fingers, and she was out there makin' the money, but then he[r assailant] got the money back from her and then raped her and beat her, and she

---

[6] While women do experience instances of police misconduct and ill (or even illegal and unethical) treatment by healthcare and social service providers, it is important to mention that untreated severe mental illness, intoxication, and other factors can contribute to negative encounters such as this one, especially when the officer or provider has a reasonable fear for his or her safety.

just got out of the hospital not too long ago, but she's back out here. We had told her last night, "why are you back? You know, you're not even fully healed." It's happened to her before, but she just keeps comin' back and she had a big'ol bottle of vodka and she was guzzling that stuff down like it was water. I think that's why they attack her and stuff, because she's just so drunk out there and y'know, talkin' to this person and that person, they seen she was weak.

Disrupted Peer Solidarity

The gendered nexus of street-based prostitution, caregiving obligations, addiction, interpersonal violence, and criminal justice system involvement creates a divisive environment that works against sustained mutual support networks among street-involved women. All of the women struggle with addictions and homelessness and most have supported others through income earned on the street. Twenty-two-year-old Monique, who is African-American, described her trajectory from factory work to street-based sex trading and caring for her common-law husband's children following his long-term incarceration in federal prison:

> The police came into my house and took my husband, and they're like, "we need social services down here 'cause we have two kids and they're not her kids" and they're like, "well if you're willing to take these kids"... I really didn't get no kind of social help when I had them. It was what made me start kind of like doing what I was doing [sex trading] 'cause I had a job at a granola factory... it was clashing and I had to quit that job. And that's when I started doing other stuff. The caseworker was like, "we gonna close this case down because you're doing everything you're supposed to be doing, they have food, your house is always clean when we come…they have everything that a kid probably would want…" My case manager closed it down. Made me feel real good, they didn't miss no school unless they was sick, that made me feel good about myself.

Like Monique, 53-year-old African-American Mary described caregiving responsibilities for children as the primary reason she worked the street while precariously housed in motels:

> I didn't want to do it, I had to do it. I had a family. When you got kids you don't want social services coming and messing with you. So you gotta make sure you got a place to stay. These motels back in them days, they was assholes. They got you sixty dollars, I had six in my family and they charged me sixty, seventy-five dollars every two days. And for a week. Mm! I had a lot of problems.

In the midst of these many responsibilities and worries, women have little time or energy left to assist their peers. Loyalties, even when successfully cultivated, can shift rapidly due to drug use and other factors, such as those described by 28-year-old African-American Nicole, who avoided working with other women following a bad experience with a street colleague she considered a friend:

> I got a gun pulled on me with her. Me and her went to this dude's house and she didn't wanna to nothin' with him, she decided she wanted to do somethin' with me. Anyway, that wasn't gonna happen, but she was more into me than she was into the dude. The dude pulled

a shotgun on us. Went to his room and pulled a shotgun out on us. I was gettin' the fuck out and after that I don't deal with her no more.

"I don't really think anybody cares about anybody out here," said 23-year-old African-American Joyce, speaking implicitly to the myriad institutional and interpersonal forces that work against the possibility of peer or neighborhood solidarity. Individuals with felony criminal convictions, for instance, cannot live with relatives in federally subsidized housing, women who have been incarcerated or homeless for extended periods often face state termination of their parental rights, and the intersections of addiction and poverty further limit the possibilities for mutual assistance. Street-involved women understandably view offers of help in this context as potentially troublesome, such that a woman who appears altruistic could demand money or favors, or be a recruiter for a pimp who does the same.

Women with relatives in the neighborhood or elsewhere in Denver face rejection from families already struggling with a number of economic burdens and incarcerated or addicted family members and loved ones. Nineteen-year-old African-American Rae felt little sympathy for a close relative who lost custody of her children:

> I have a aunty that does that and you see her go up and down the street in this area a lot. It's crazy. But she said one guy beated her. She got in the car with him, he beated her, choked her, almost killed her. She thought it was cute, I guess, she told my whole family, and they were just devastated, and they don't want nothin' to do with her, because she can't build a straight life. She have five kids that she need to attend to that got taken away by Human Services and she don't care about. All she care about is the street.

In the absence of sustained social support from peers and family members who face considerable constraints of their own, some women report giving up entirely. As 26-year-old Kay, who is White, concisely put it, "my kids were taken away from me a year ago, that's why I'm out on the street."

Limited Information Sharing with Healthcare Providers and Peers

Women's knowledge of statutes, police procedure, and the criminal justice system more generally is partial and incomplete, resulting in hypervigilance and consequent restricted information sharing with healthcare providers as well as peers. Uniformed police officers are always present in urban US emergency rooms, the primary care provider for most street-involved women. Many women believe that healthcare providers share sensitive information with criminal justice professionals, a perception that leads to healthcare avoidance; as 50-year-old Deb, who is White, noted with respect to women who need medical attention, "you got warrants you better suck it in." Jacinta, a Latina in her early 50s, noted, "I was treated pretty, pretty bad…being on drugs and stuff. They don't like that…I try to stay away from'em…it just seems like they're angry, like I'm nothing 'cause I'm on drugs."

Anne, a 30-year-old nurse in Denver's busiest and largest inner city emergency room, provided her perspective on encounters with individuals who appeared to be seeking prescription narcotics for their own use or to resell to others, which frustrated her due to the number of people in her own family and social circle who could not afford to visit a healthcare provider:

> You have this person coming in, they have no health insurance, like there's people you know who have health insurance and can't afford to see the doctor…And they're coming in to get like, free morphine and dilaudid [a narcotic pain reliever]…it does make you generalize… Sometimes me and my coworkers feel like we're not doing anything for them…we're just giving them meds which replaces their habit.

This perspective, while derived from Anne's own experiences, helps to explain the complex reasons that women may restrict their information sharing with providers. Women monitor what they share with peers for different reasons, but the criminalization of their illicit drug use and sex trading activities are foremost among these; as 40-year-old Marisol, a Latina, noted, "it's illegal, so you can't trust no one out there." Notably interviews with women in neighborhood motel rooms mirrored this sentiment, such that while women freely disclosed about their activities related to drug use and prostitution, they consistently talked about an aunty, friend, or acquaintance when they described violent incidents, instead choosing to depict themselves as sufficiently streetwise to avoid victimization.

The hypervigilance that necessarily accompanies street involvement creates a divisive social environment in which women must remain attuned to a social cues in order to avoid retribution, arrest, or other undesirable involvement with those who 31-year-old Native American Sandy noted with respect to the limited likelihood of peer assistance in a crisis, "like to get in your business and then, 'if I go down, I go down alone.'" Thirty-three-year-old Angie, who is White, said that the social environment in which street-based prostitution takes place creates a number of challenges:

> I've met a few girls that I've gotten close with, but you're always in competition no matter what, you know? Somebody's gonna take a date of yours or they look better than you. There's jealousy involved. And if the other girls have pimps, then you're kind of putting yourself in danger if you don't have somebody looking out for you.

Street-involved women must also limit or otherwise carefully monitor what they share with others because of their status as highly desirable police informants regarding the drug and gang activities they regularly witness. Twenty-three-year-old African-American NeNe, whose family is intergenerationally involved in prostitution as both sex workers and intermediaries, described the delicate balance inherent in maintaining good, and potentially even beneficial, relations with police, who value the information street-involved women might share with them:

> We know every detail of Colfax from anywhere, y'know what I'm sayin'? Because we walk, and when you're in a car you pass that shit up, you just don't recognize nothing like that…you got some real cops, they know what's going down. Keep it one hundred with them, they keep it one hundred with you.

Health Diagnosis in Crisis Contexts and the Criminalization of HIV Status

Diagnoses women receive often occur in the emergency room or in jail, where women's health is compromised by recent drug use, sleep deprivation, long-term inadequate nutrition, untreated health conditions, and the trauma that often surrounds events leading to arrest and incarceration. All of these factors compromise diagnoses' integrity and present challenges as providers attempt to assess a woman who appears to be delusional, paranoid, or otherwise unstable, symptoms which may result from prolonged substance abuse, fear of an abuser, an untreated mental illness, or all of these things. Maria, a 28-year-old Latina case manager, described facing this reality when a man murdered one of her clients, who he believed had infected him with HIV, noting, "it was this realization of, 'oh, the world really wasn't a safe place for you.'"

Recognizing the frequency with which crisis context diagnosis takes place, women frequently use the term "jail meds" as a general reference term for medications prescribed in correctional facilities to treat anxiety, depression, and schizoaffective disorders, some of which emerge from the traumatic experience of incarceration itself. Thirty-two-year-old Kelly, who is White, described jail meds as a control mechanism correctional facility staff use to ensure compliance:

> They put everybody...I don't care what type of stuff you're on in the outside...they would substitute it for whatever they have at the jail...and up the dose...just to keep you...sane... give them way crazy meds and then it's just like they are a bunch of walking zombies...So they don't get out of control.

Once released from jail, women arrested on prostitution-related charges receive a 30 day prescription for medications they received while incarcerated and must comply with a court-issued health order, which includes a mandatory HIV test, at Denver's largest hospital. Women who test HIV positive may face a felony conviction if arrested again on a prostitution-related charge, which is an ambivalent subject for street-involved women. Forty-one-year-old White Carrie, for instance, shared a cell in prison with a woman she felt deserved the 2-year sentence she had received following her felony conviction under the Colorado statute "Prostitution with Knowledge of AIDS." Conversely, women who disclosed their HIV positive status to me often emphasized how this systematic disenfranchisement through criminalization of their transactional sexual and drug use activities as well as their health status contributes directly to further health problems, both for themselves and others. As 49-year-old African-American Toni put it, some street-involved women living with HIV "just don't give a fuck...when I started feeling that, that wasn't a good feeling...because every time that I had a trick who wanted to do it without a condom, I didn't give a fuck, and he didn't give a fuck."

Discussion

All three case studies demonstrate that criminalization increases the likelihood that women who sell or trade sex will experience violence and third party exploitation. Criminalization likewise decreases women's abilities to collectively organize and protect their health and safety. Each of the research sites, despite their unique cultural contexts, features remarkably similar accounts of the multiple forms of violence and systemic marginalization that women experience as a result of criminalization. It is particularly evident that the key risks posed to women's health and safety emerge *not* from selling or trading sex, but rather from the exclusionary conditions created by criminalization.

The criminal justice system plays a pervasive role in the women's lives by positioning them as criminal perpetrators and public health threats in ways that facilitate the deployment of violence against them at several levels. Examples presented throughout this chapter illustrate how criminalization creates and reinforces numerous forms of structurally mediated exclusion in women's interactions with the criminal justice system, healthcare providers, clients, and various actors they rely upon to engage in extrajudicial problem-solving measures in lieu of police assistance. Women in all three case studies live, work, and spend most of their time in the neighborhoods or venues where they sell or trade sex, which increases the totalizing impacts of such violence by embedding them in a socioeconomic context dominated by illicit or criminalized activities.

The socio-legal denial of women's capacities to earn an income via transactional sex is itself a very troubling illustration of the injustice associated with the criminalization of sex work and the inequity with regard to the women's protection and safety under the law relative to other citizens. Women who sell or trade sex know that they are criminal justice system targets, and they accordingly spend a significant amount of their time attempting to avoid police detection and arrest. This often compromises their abilities to screen clients, use condoms, or otherwise ensure their safety by exerting control in the transactional sexual exchange. Criminalization likewise increases violence, exploitation, and other forms of abuse the women face from police, clients, intermediaries, and figures that exercise control over the criminalized socioeconomic environment in which they live and work. This socio-legal and spatial exclusion places women at the mercy of those who control the context in which they sell or trade sex, whether it is an indoor venue such as a Chinese hostess bar managed by powerful gangsters or a North American street scene dominated by the illicit drug economy.

Women's highly desirable status as informants due to their often extensive knowledge of other criminalized activities encourages police patrol officers or higher-ranked criminal justice system professionals to elicit information from them. This sometimes occurs in exchange for freedom from correctional control, a reduced sentence, or, in the Canadian case study, financial incentives. Yet women who agree to these terms by providing information about prominent figures in the illicit drug trade or other criminalized entrepreneurial ventures risk violent retribution for violating prevailing cultural codes that restrict information sharing with outsiders.

Women also experience physical and sexual violence from numerous actors who play prominent roles in their lives, including police officers, gang members, and third parties who profit from their sex trading. This violence occurs in conjunction with a lack of social supports or legal recourse to help women deal with sexually transmitted infections, clients who refuse to pay or who otherwise abuse them, and other concerns directly related to sex trading. Women are highly cognizant of how these multiple forms of violence operate in their lives, whether in the form of systemic exclusion from healthcare, constant fear of arrest, or clients who believe they can assault them with impunity.

Purveyors of controlled substances, madams, gang members, and other powerful actors engaged in criminalized activities all variously benefit from women's sexual labor. Since prostitution is part of the broader criminalized economy in which they operate, women who sell or trade sex must engage with individuals whose activities make them of interest to police as potential informants and provide additional grounds for issuing women with more serious criminal charges. Women likewise become subject to the extrajudicial, and often violent, problem solving that characterizes the illicit drug economy and related criminalized activities. Case studies presented here paint a vivid portrait of women who must navigate their relationships with these opposing forces while managing their own struggles with family members, intimate partners, clients, and, in the North American case studies, addictions and related health problems.

The fraught conditions in which the women earn an income, combined with competition for clients and other resources, and the social stigma and temporality that many women associate with sex trading activities, discourage women from collective rights-based organizing. The women have numerous financial and caregiving obligations to family members and loved ones that limit the amount of emotional energy and time they can share with their peers, who are often dealing with their own similar struggles. In the absence of solidarity, women experience further social isolation, stigmatization, and vulnerability to relationships with individuals who may further exploit them under the guise of offering protection and companionship.

Women delay or avoid healthcare as a result of stigmatizing treatment, high costs, and concerns about possible connections between criminal justice, healthcare, and social service professionals. This results from the generalized climate of fear and paranoia criminalization creates for those engaged in behaviors targeted by legislation, which is only heightened for women subject to criminal justice scrutiny for other reasons. Most hostesses in China, for instance, lack the requisite residence permit that would allow them to legally reside in an urban area and accordingly can only earn an income in economic sectors willing to disregard this requirement. North American street-involved women's dual stigmatization and criminalization as illicit drug users and sexual service providers likewise dramatically impact their abilities to protect their health and safety.

Women's perceptions of their healthcare access may sharply differ from those of healthcare or social service providers, often because the women's experiences have shown them that the world is an unfair place characterized by arbitrary rule enforcement against which they have limited or no legal or other recourse. This is particularly evident in instances where police officers confiscate condoms as evidence of women's engagement in prostitution-related activities. Police patrol officers are street-level bureaucrats tasked with the very challenging task of implementing law and public policy in conditions where they must rapidly make decisions in response to citizen complaints. Like the criminal justice professionals who prosecute, adjudicate, and monitor the women's criminal cases, patrol officers find it difficult to distinguish prostitution from legal forms of heteronormative sociosexual interaction. This police difficulty identifying a woman who may be exchanging sex for money results in the confiscation of condoms as evidence of a woman's intent to engage in prostitution and consequently reduces women's abilities to protect themselves and their clients from sexually transmitted infections. As the next chapter will illustrate, these significant risks to women's health and safety are part of socio-legally entrenched restrictions on their citizenship and autonomy.

References

Bates, J., and R. Berg. 2014. Sex Workers as Safe Sex Advocates: Sex Workers Protect Both Themselves and the Wider Community from HIV. *AIDS Education and Prevention* 26(3): 191–201.

Bernstein, E. 2007. *Temporarily Yours: Intimacy, Authenticity, and the Commerce of Sex*. Chicago: University of Chicago Press.

Blankenship, K., and S. Koester. 2002. Criminal Law, Policing Policy and HIV Risk in Female Sex Workers and Injection Drug Users. *The Journal of Law, Medicine and Ethics* 30: 548–559.

Cameron, S. 2010. *On the Farm: Robert William Pickton and the Tragic Story of Vancouver's Missing Women*. Toronto: Knopf.

Crago, A. 2009. *Arrest the Violence: Human Rights Abuses Against Sex Workers in Central and Eastern Europe and Central Asia*. New York: Open Society Foundations. http://www.opensocietyfoundations.org/sites/default/files/arrest-violence-20091217.pdf.

Denver Police Department. 2015. *2015 Crime Statistics & Maps*. http://www.denvergov.org/police/PoliceDepartment/CrimeInformation/CrimeStatisticsMaps/tabid/441370/Default.aspx.

Donovan, B., C. Harcourt, S. Egger, and C. Fairley. 2010. Improving the Health of Sex Workers in NSW: Maintaining Success. *NSW Public Health Bulletin* 21(3–4): 74–77.

Fischer, B., J. Rehm, S. Brissette, S. Brochu, J. Bruneau, N. El-Guebaly, L. Noel, M. Tyndall, C. Wild, P. Mun, and D. Baliunas. 2005. Illicit Opioid Use in Canada: Comparing Social, Health, and Drug Use Characteristics of Untreated Users in Five Cities (OPICAN Study). *Journal of Urban Health* 82(2): 250–266.

Frank, K. 2002. *G-strings and Sympathy: Strip Club Regulars and Male Desire*. Durham, NC: Duke University Press.

Gomes, T., M. Mamdani, I. Dhalla, S. Cornish, J. Paterson, and D. Jurrlink. 2014. The Burden of Premature Opioid-Related Mortality. *Addiction* 109(9): 1482–1488.

Harcourt, C., J. Connor, S. Egger, C. Fairley, H. Wand, M. Chen, L. Marshall, J. Kaldor, and B. Donovan. 2010. The Decriminalization of Sex Work Is Associated with Better Coverage of Health Promotion Programs for Sex Workers. *The Australian and New Zealand Journal of Public Health* 34(5): 482–486.

References

Jeffrey, L., and G. MacDonald. 2006. *Sex Workers in the Maritimes Talk Back*. Vancouver: University of British Columbia Press.

Jenkins, C., the Cambodian Prostitutes' Union, Women's Network for Unity, and C. Sainsbury. 2006. *Violence and Exposure to HIV Among Sex Workers in Phnom Penh, Cambodia*. Washington, DC: POLICY Project/USAID. http://www.hivpolicy.org/Library/HPP001702.pdf.

Kerrigan, D., P. Telles, H. Torres, C. Overs, and C. Castle. 2008. Community Development and HIV/STI-Related Vulnerability Among Female Sex Workers in Rio de Janeiro, Brazil. *Health Education Research* 23(1): 137–145.

O'Brien, J. 2015. Ice Storm—Emergencies Soar as Crystal Meth's Use in London Becomes Rampant. *London Free Press*, May 2. http://www.lfpress.com/2015/05/01/emergencies-soar-as-crystal-meths-use-here-becomes-rampant.

Office of Police Integrity. 2008. Interacting with Sex Workers: A Good Practice Guide and Self-Check. Victoria, Australia: Office of Police Integrity. http://www.ibac.vic.gov.au/docs/default-source/opi-prevention-and-education/interacting-with-sexworkers---a-good-practice-guide-and-self-check---november-2008.pdf?sfvrsn=2.

Office of State Council. 2012. *Aizibing shierwu cingdou jihua/AIDS Twelve Five Actions Proposal*. Beijing: Office of State Council of China.

Orchard, T., S. Farr, S. Macphail, C. Wender, and C. Wilson. 2014. Expanding the Scope of Inquiry: Exploring Accounts of Childhood and Family Among Canadian Sex Workers. *Canadian Journal of Human Sexuality* 23(1): 9–18.

Overs, C., and K. Hawkins. 2011. Can Rights Stop the Wrongs? Exploring the Connections Between Framings of Sex Workers' Rights and Sexual and Reproductive Health. *BMC International Health and Human Rights* 11(Suppl 3): S6.

Overs, C., and B. Loff. 2013. The Tide Cannot Be Turned Without Us: Sex Workers and the Global Response to HIV. *Journal of the International AIDS Society* 16: 1–6.

Pan, S., and Y. Huang. 2011. Evaluation of the Effect of 2010 Massive Police Raids (2010 Nian Dasaohuang Xiaoguo de Pinggu). In *Rights and Multidimension: Essays from the Third International Symposium on Sexual Research in China* (Quanli Yu Duoyuan: Disanjie Xingyanjiu Guoji Yantaohui Lunwenji). Beijing: The Center for Disease Control.

Redwood, R. 2013. Myths and Realities of Male Sex Work: A Personal Perspective. In *Selling Sex: Experience, Advocacy, and Research on Sex Work in Canada*, ed. E. van der Meulen, E. Durisin, and V. Love, 45–57. Vancouver: University of British Columbia Press.

Rekart, M. 2005. Sex-Work Harm Reduction. *Lancet* 366: 2123–2134.

Rosenbaum, M. 1981. *Women on Heroin*. New Brunswick, NJ: Rutgers University Press.

Sanders, T. 2005. "It's Just Acting": Sex Workers' Strategies for Capitalizing on Sexuality. *Gender, Work & Organization* 12(4): 319–342.

Scheper-Hughes, N. 1992. *Death Without Weeping: The Violence of Everyday Life in Brazil*. Berkeley: University of California Press.

Scorgie, F., K. Vasey, E. Harper, M. Richter, P. Nare, S. Maseko, and M. Chersich. 2013. Human Rights Abuses and Collective Resilience Among Sex Workers in Four African Countries: A Qualitative Study. *Globalization & Health* 9: 1–13.

Shannon, K., and J. Csete. 2010. Violence, Condom Negotiation, and HIV/STI Risk Among Sex Workers. *JAMA, the Journal of the American Medical Association* 304(5): 573–574.

Shields, A. 2012. *Criminalizing Condoms: How Policing Practices Put Sex Workers and HIV Services at Risk in Kenya, Namibia, Russia, South Africa, the United States, and Zimbabwe*. New York: The Sexual Health & Rights Project of the Open Society Foundations.

Smarajit, J., I. Basu, M. Rotheram-Borus, and P. Newman. 2004. The Sonagachi Project: A Sustainable Community Intervention Program. *AIDS Education & Prevention* 16(5): 405–414.

UNAIDS (Joint United Nations Programme on HIV/AIDS). 2012. *UNAIDS Guidance Note on HIV & Sex Work*. Geneva: UNAIDS. http://www.unaids.org/sites/default/files/sub_landing/files/JC2306_UNAIDS-guidance-note-HIV-sex-work_en.pdf.

Wen, J. 2006. *Aizibing fangzhi tiaoli (Laws on AIDS Prevention)*. Beijing: Office of State Council of China.

Wurth, M., R. Schleifer, M. McLemore, K. Todrys, and J. Amon. 2013. Condoms as Evidence of Prostitution in the United States and the Criminalization of Sex Work. *Journal of the International AIDS Society* 16(1): 18626–18628.
Xie, H. 2010. Sex Workers on Leash were Paraded in Dongwan/Dongwan maiyinnv zaoshengqian shizhong. *Guangzhou Daily/Guangzhou Ribao* 27: 2.
Zheng, T. 2009a. *Red Lights: The Lives of Sex Workers in Postsocialist China*. Minneapolis: University of Minnesota Press.
_____. 2009b. *Ethnographies of Prostitution in Contemporary China: Gender Relations, HIV/AIDS, and Nationalism*. New York: Palgrave Macmillan Press.

Chapter 3
Negotiating Systematic Collusion: Autonomy, Citizenship, and Resistance

Sex Workers' Negotiations of the Exclusionary Regime

The previous two chapters explored the different adversarial relationships that flow from the criminalization of sex work, including those with people in the criminal justice and healthcare systems, other authority figures, and their clients. These relationships often reinforce the women's marginalized socioeconomic and political status and also limit their abilities to collectively organize themselves around health and legal issues while further inhibiting their access to housing, legal employment, and government benefits. While disproportionate power and authority is concentrated in the criminal justice system and other institutions at state and municipal levels, women in sex work employ a range of pragmatic adaptive strategies with which to circumvent the structural violence and marginalization they experience under criminalization. These strategies are complex, context dependent, sometimes specific to individual women, and do not erase the many dangers involved with trading or selling sex. Yet despite these realities, it is essential to explore the ways in which the women struggle with and juggle the systemic constraints involved in doing work that is criminalized yet meaningful within the context of their lives and essential to their survival.

One of the key strategies employed is avoiding police arrest. Women's approaches in this context vary by the venue and areas in which they work and how visible their activities are to the public. Those doing street-based sex work develop strategies that are unique compared to their indoor counterparts because of their high visibility in public or open spaces. Dewey and St. Germain (2014) observed that far from being reactive or ad hoc responses to immediate danger, the strategies developed by women in their US street-based field site capitalize upon and reflect their in-depth knowledge of policing practices and the behaviors of individual patrol officers working the local strolls. These strategies included soliciting in a subdued manner, using respectful language with officers, avoiding public involvement in other criminalized activities, and using knowledge about police procedure gleaned from previous encounters to avoid future arrests. Other street-involved women indicate that they try to ensure that their clients park in particular spots that are removed from intense police surveillance and ask them different questions to ascertain whether or not they are undercover police officers (Bruckert and Parent 2013). Women may also adjust their bodily comportment and street-based activities so they are more indicative of panhandling or other behaviors generally regarded as more innocuous than solicitation (Bourgois and Schonberg 2009).

Outdoor and indoor sex venues may overlap in criminalized sex work settings and the policing of street activities can lead clients who formerly patronized street-involved women to shift to indoor sex workers' services to avoid arrest, as research conducted on online forum posts by men who buy sex in ten US cities found (Holt et al. 2014). Like their peers on the street, women who work indoors develop arrest avoidance strategies based on their own experiences, what they learn from others, and the sociosexual, legal, and interpersonal conditions that structure their working environments. Sanders's (2005) work in the UK identified several such strategies, including forging good relationships with neighboring residents or businesses, moving to different locales to work, and having alibis and cover stories prepared in the event of police raids or inquiries. Bruckert and Law (2013) examined an array of approaches used to avoid police arrest, which were adopted by women in sex work and those who occupy different positions in the hierarchy of agencies and groups of individuals who make up third party members in indoor sex work in Canada. Among them were the careful selection of the number and kinds of establishments managed by the same agency or person, establishing businesses that fall under different licensing categories (i.e., body rub parlors, holistic health centers, or massage parlors), and being very cautious about the distribution of profits from indoor sex work in different kinds of accounts and financial institutions.

Cultivating regular clients with familiar preferences and personalities can also help women negotiate their safety and avoid the threat of police arrest or presence. Women interpret their relationships with clients, both regular and otherwise, in ways that reflect both the cultural norms and gendered economic constraints that shape their lives. In some instances their relationships with regulars can closely resemble intimate partnerships not immediately associated with transactional sex. Women who trade sex for money in Malawi, for instance, describe their activities using the term *chibwenzi*, which refers to a culturally sanctioned intimate premarital relationship that involves the exchange of sex for money (Tavory and Poulin 2012). Nigerian sex workers likewise report their willingness to engage in condom-less sex with affluent clients who, in providing them with more money, mitigate the everyday economic struggles they face (Izugbara 2007).

Developing strategies related to the acquisition of healthcare services is another important domain in which women in the sex trade have to negotiate and often resist the stigmatization and criminalization under which they work. As a result of unaffordable costs, lengthy travel times, and fear of stigmatizing treatment or punitive sanctions, women are often forced to negotiate their self-care through shared knowledge gained through peer consultation with other women in the trade. Sex workers in Guatemala, for instance, express frustration with healthcare providers who, in addition to stigmatizing treatment, expected payment or treatment with prescription drugs they could not afford (Porras et al. 2008). Due to the travel distance, high costs, wait times, and poor care at healthcare clinics and hospitals, Tanzanian sex workers eat a plant-based and high protein diet, wash with antiseptic solution after sex, and only seek out medical care when presented with symptoms of illness (Outwater et al. 2001).

Hostesses and other sex industry workers in Liuzhou, China, dismiss public health literature as irrelevant to their lives, and report eschewing condoms with regular clients, regular vaginal douching and relying upon peers and the Internet for sexual health advice (Youchun et al. 2014). A study in Uzbekistan, where women who sell sex risk being reported to police if they seek healthcare at a clinic, found that more than half of the women self-treated their sexually transmitted infections and continued to work while treatment was ongoing (Alibayeva et al. 2007). Likewise, 97 % of Tijuana injection drug users self-treated their abscesses, usually by applying aloe vera, a rag soaked in salt water, taking penicillin over the counter, and other self-administered draining and cleaning measures (Pollini et al. 2010).

In addition to using various forms of self-care to manage their health, many women in sex work rely on insights, knowledge, and supports they glean from one another to increase their safety and foster solidarity among themselves. In Nairobi, Kenya, women share mobile phone numbers with one another so they can call upon their peers for bail money when arrested on prostitution charges, and gather information about taxi drivers, night watchmen, and other figures with observational knowledge regarding policing-related activities (Izugbara 2011). Sex workers in Swaziland with similar relationships of trust, solidarity, and providing mutual aid to other sex workers reported a greater likelihood of using condoms with clients more consistently, testing for HIV, and facing less discrimination (Fonner et al. 2014). Likewise in Karnataka, India, women who belong to a sex worker collective have an increased likelihood of condom use with paid partners (Halli et al. 2006). These selective social bonds derive from geographic provenance as well as the work venue or identification as a sex worker more generally. In China, women who migrate from rural areas to work in sex industry venues provide critical support in counseling peers from the same town or area about condom use, violence mitigation, general social support, and health seeking (Tucker et al. 2011).

The sex workers' rights movement is a larger-scale and formalized version of the selective mutual aid that sex workers provide to one another, and it has yielded significant legal and socioeconomic changes in the lives of sex workers globally. It emerged in the 1970s as part of the international women's movement and was rooted in sex workers' frustration with various feminist groups, namely radical and predominantly White feminists, who condemned prostitution as a sexist expression of male dominance and yet claimed to have the authority to speak "for" women in the sex trade (Leigh 1997). Over time these loosely united and necessarily context-specific mobilizations for the recognition of sexual labor as work took institutional forms, as in the case of the St. James Infirmary in San Francisco, the only US healthcare clinic tailored to sex workers' needs (Majic 2013) and the formation of labor unions for sex industry workers in Australia, New Zealand, Germany, the Netherlands, and Canada (Gall 2006; Lopez-Embury and Sanders 2009).

These activist groups can also be virtual, like the Network of Sex Work Projects, whose Web site unites information and resources from more than 150 sex workers' rights groups in over 60 countries with the goal of supporting self-organization by sex workers and opposing criminalization (www.nwsp.org/members). Sex workers' rights groups provide support to sex workers through collective action, such as unionization, as well as developing strategies to combat everyday discrimination. For instance a sex workers' rights groups in Andhra Pradesh, India, responded to police harassment by developing an "enforcement pyramid," which consisted of developing collective strategies to question the police regarding their grounds for arrest and providing helpful information that women could use to file written complaints and proceed with court challenges regarding unjust police action (Rao Biradavolu et al. 2009).

Sex workers can encounter difficulties in finding legal work when faced with criminal records, gaps in work histories, and being forced to hide their sex work activities (Sanders 2007). Some women confront these restrictions by capitalizing on their experiential knowledge to take on a managerial sex industry role that offers more power, control, and income with less invasive client contact than prostitution. For instance, Nigerian madams in Palermo, Sicily, all previously exchanged sex for money and use their knowledge of the business to socialize newly arrived young migrants, who pay madams substantial sums of money for accommodation and other costs, some of which could be characterized as debt bondage (Cole 2006).

Likewise, a street-involved woman who works together with other women for an intermediary may aspire to the increased respect, greater authority, and more limited sex-for-money exchanges involved in "bottom bitch" status, which involves her working as the intermediary's personnel manager (Weinkauf 2010; Williamson and Cluse-Tolar 2002). These activities may provide a woman with more money and status while demanding less physically invasive client contact, yet managing other women's sexual labor could result in heavier criminal sanctions for pimping, trafficking, or related offenses. As with the other strategies the women employ to negotiate social exclusion, such choices come at a potentially high cost.

Case Study One: China

Hostesses resist and negotiate constraints on their autonomy and citizenship through strategies designed to protect themselves, avoid arrest, and achieve upward social mobility. They do this by developing protective relationships with gangsters, forming temporary alliances, retaining regular customers, and striving for the upward mobility that they hope will make them full-fledged, legitimate urbanites.

Protection Networks

In the absence of legal protections, hostesses found it imperative to form protective social networks with gangsters who could protect them from violence inflicted by bar bouncers, clients, and other gangsters. Every experienced hostess I met during my research fostered relationships with one or two gangsters who they provided with free sexual services in exchange for protection. Hostesses at Romantic Dreams with protective ties to gangsters were able to leave the bar and work somewhere else without suffering the bar bouncer's violence. Hostesses who did not have such relationships with gangsters, however, did not dare to leave the bar, and hence novice hostesses gradually learned to form such relationships.

Hostess Wu was favored by a neighboring bar's bouncer and felt compelled to develop a relationship with him. She told me,

> In my hometown, nobody dares to touch me because I have a wide network of friends. It's so different here. Here I don't have anyone. No one cares if I am bullied or abused. I can't seek redress or justice anywhere because I am a hostess! He is a thug. He is local. I have to be good to him. I need someone to turn to when I encounter trouble on this street.

Wu called upon this bouncer for help whenever clients or members of a different gang harassed her, and he never failed to arrive with a team of gangsters to assault the source of Wu's troubles. Wu also formed a relationship with a bar owner as a backup, knowing that the illegal status of her work left her with no support in the city other than these men. Many other hostesses also managed to form relationships with bar owners, bouncers, or skilled street fighters and frequently joked, "we hostesses are relatives of the underworld."

Temporary Alliances

Despite the internal competition and at times, outright denial of affiliation with other women working at hostess bars, hostesses did sometimes form temporary alliances in small groups based on blood relations and place of origin. Members of these small cliques not only offered advice and suggestions in dealing with clients and boyfriends but also provided emotional, professional, physical, and economic support to one another. Each of the three karaoke bars I worked in had biological sisters who came to the city together and worked in the same bar as hostesses. At Romantic Dreams, hostess Dee enlisted her gangster networks to ensure the safety of her 17-year-old sister Bai, while also teaching her how to protect herself against drunk and aggressive clients. She took her to beauty salons and shopping markets to get fancy clothes and an appealing hairstyle, and when Bai fell in love with a client, Dee was there for her, offering advice and emotional support.

Some hostesses either came to the city with their relatives or were later reunited with relatives after they worked in the bars. It was not uncommon for hostesses to find cousins working as hostesses in the same or other bars in the city. Hostess Tan ran into her cousin Wen on the street in the city and learned that Wen was working as a hostess in a nearby sauna bar. While in the village, the two had harbored years of animosity against each other, in Dalian they overcame their misgivings and strategically formed a temporary alliance based on the exchange of benefits. When Tan had nowhere to go following her return from a trip to Shanghai, Wen took her in and allowed her to share her living space with her roommates.

While consanguinity served as the foundation for a more permanent coalition, alliances built upon hostesses' places of origin and the exchange of mutual benefits could be equally strong. Hostesses in a clique not only supported the interests of the group members but also introduced one another to new jobs in more upscale bars. For instance, Hong and Ling were in a clique, from which they each benefited a great deal. When Hong's regular client introduced Hong to a madam in an upscale bar who offered her a job, Hong brought Ling over to meet the madam and managed to enable Ling to work there as well. In this alliance, Hong was happy because she was able to rely on Ling for emotional support in this completely new and daunting environment of the upscale bar. Ling, too, was thrilled because she was able to enter an upscale bar and earn more money.

In such alliances, hostesses did deeply care about one another and guard each other's interests. When a hostess's boyfriend abandoned or cheated on her, her allies would always come to comfort her and support her through the emotional crisis. At times, hostesses in an alliance mobilized their efforts to resist certain clients' mistreatment or abuse of their hostess colleagues. For instance, when hostess Han's client lover mistreated her, Dee and several other hostesses in Han's alliance organized a group that admonished him and demanded an apology for Han. Pressured by all these women, he finally did. In another instance, hostess Chen was distraught when she found her client lover having sex with another woman in a sauna bar. Friends in her coalition took her out to eat and drink in restaurants and then to dance at a disco bar all night to take her mind away from her client lover. Everyone advised her to forget him and focus on earning money from other clients, and Chen later did follow their advice and overcame the angst.

At times, hostesses in a coalition rose up together in defiance against exploitation in bar operations. During my research in Romantic Dreams, at one time, the male madam only led his girlfriend May and her close friends into karaoke rooms for clients' selection. This was unfair to other hostesses who had been suffering financial losses due to the lack of customers. Hostess Hui approached the male madam, interrogating him on behalf of the other hostesses: "Didn't you know that some hostesses had not had any clients for several days? Why did you just push your girlfriend and her friend into the room without informing the rest of the hostesses, especially when your girlfriend had already had clients tonight! Why didn't you lead the other hostesses into the room to be chosen?"

Hearing her words, the male madam jumped up from his chair, punching her in the face and head with his fists, kicking her in the chest and belly, yelling, "Didn't you already have clients? Why are you minding the other hostesses' business? None of the others complained. So why are you complaining about me having my girlfriend sit in the karaoke room?" While Hui was beaten into a chair, hostesses from her alliance threw themselves in front of her, using their bodies to form a shield to protect her from the madam's blows and kicks. Together, they asked the madam to stop the abuse, and then he did.

In this case, one hostess protested against the madam's injustice, followed by the support of many other hostesses in her clique. Despite the positive effect and occasional triumph of hostesses' informal networks, it is noteworthy that the alliance based on native place and exchange of benefits was often temporary, subject to dissolution. These cliques' ephemeral nature stemmed from the competition between hostesses for scarce resources, the disaffiliation with the group, and the ultimate betrayal of group members. The complaint I heard the most about the other hostesses was the lack of loyalty. Hostess Lin, for instance, had been in a clique with Mei because the two came from the same rural place, yet when Lin fell sick in the aftermath of a painful abortion, Mei abandoned her and did not come to see her or help her out. Lin lamented that during the time when she was hospitalized, she was by herself and felt bitterly alone, and after that incident, Lin ended her friendship with Mei.

In another example of a fleeting and unstable clique, Chen ended her friendship with Hai after Hai offered her an insultingly small amount of money (200 yuan, approximately US$30) in appreciation for the time she spent helping her heal from an abortion. The friendship between hostesses Huang and Dong, who provided each other with emotional support, ended when Dong stole Huang's client. Such limitations and constraints on hostesses' friendships stemmed from the substantial costs associated with collective actions or resistance. Were hostesses to mobilize together to defend their rights as full citizens, they would have to publicize their sex work identity and subject themselves to stigma and police arrest, which would severely circumvent their aspiration of leaving sex work eventually and climbing the social ladder. Hostesses were thus caught in the constant tension between loyalty toward their group and the allure of potential benefits that could result from breaking away from the group. In a system that criminalizes sex work, collective resistance would only invite political repression and political punishment. Hence it is unsurprising that hostesses' temporary supportive coalitions stopped short of collective resistance.

Contractual Relationships with Regular Clients

Hostesses preferred to enter into contractual relationships with regular clients as a means to avoid arrest during police raids. In such a relationship, hostesses left the bar to reside in a clandestine apartment rented by the clients. The client provided monthly payments, gifts, entertainment fees, assorted amenities, and all the living expenses to the hostess, in exchange for her exclusive sexual service to him. During the agreed-upon contractual time, the hostess was obligated to terminate all sexual relations with other men and discontinue her work in the bar. The hidden place and the clandestine nature of sex work in this contractual relationship could help hostesses evade police harassment, police arrests, and other risks and violence from random clients. As I have discussed elsewhere (Zheng 2009b), condom-less sex was normal in such contractual relationship for the two parties to convey trust, loyalty, intimacy, and freedom from diseases. While hostesses would be more likely to choose this kind of underground and concealed form of sex work to ensure their safety from police harassment and police arrest, unfortunately, the practice of avoiding condom use necessitated by this relationship potentially exposed them to sexually transmitted infections.

Urban Citizenship

Hostesses used sex work as a stepping stone to transform from second-class rural migrants to first-class urban citizens. Only 4 out of the 200 hostesses I worked with came from cities and the rest were rural migrant women. In China, rural migrant women are institutionally, culturally, and socially discriminated against via the deeply entrenched rural–urban apartheid system. The household registration system has divided China's population into permanent urban "citizens" who hold urban residence permits and rural/migrant people who do not. Rural migrants' lack of urban residence permits denies them subsidized housing, healthcare, employment, children's education, and other benefits associated with state-sanctioned urban residency (Zheng 2009a).

Rural migrants to Dalian must meet a number of requirements to obtain an urban residence permits, including a legitimate, stable job in the center district of the city, a state-recognized university degree, or a 5-year contract with a company located outside the center zone but within the boundaries of the new zone or the satellite zone (Zheng 2015). Rural migrants who are not able to meet these requirements are required to purchase either an apartment worth at least 800,000 yuan (US$129,032) or a commercial building worth at least one million yuan (US$161,290) in the center zone in order to apply for the urban resident permit. In addition, banks inflict severe loan and mortgage restrictions on rural migrants, but not on urbanites. Anyone who marries a person who holds an urban residence permit is still required to purchase an apartment in the city and wait 8 years before being allowed to apply for urban residence (Zheng 2015).

For rural migrant hostesses who lacked marketable skills and were doomed to low-wage jobs in factories, restaurants, and houses as domestic maids, sex work offered them the most profits with the least investment and an expedient way to be transformed into the urban identity. To hostesses, sex work was the royal road to achieve their goals, as it was not uncommon for government officials to illegally issue their hostess lovers urban resident permits and transform these hostesses' rural migrant second-class status. For instance, hostess Yu's regular client was a government official, who issued her an urban household registration permit for free. Yu, while showing me her urban resident permit, proudly called herself "a very successful woman who is now a full-fledged first-class urbanite."

A large number of hostesses I knew were either married to or kept by wealthy clients as wives or mistresses, which allowed them to eventually became not only urbanites with an urban resident permit, but also entrepreneurial owners of businesses such as gift shops, butcher shops, sauna bars, hotels, and restaurants. Some hostesses left the bars and worked in their own businesses bought for them by their wealthy husbands or client lovers, and I conducted interviews with several of them in their own businesses. Hostess Han, for instance, was married to her client who was a manager of a prestigious hotel in the city. Prior to the marriage, Han earned enough money to purchase a house for her family in her rural hometown and another one for herself in the city, and she singlehandedly supported her parents and seven siblings. After she married, she ran an import–export business that her husband bought for her. Now she lives as a full-fledged first-class urban citizen in Beijing with her husband and her child.

Likewise, hostess Yu worked in a low-tier bar until one of her clients helped her find work in an upscale bar where she met a client who kept her as his mistress for 5 years. During these 5 years, he bought her a spacious apartment in the center of Shanghai, where real estate costs were skyrocketing, as well as a small company for her to own and run. He also gave her money to go to college and get a university degree in elementary education. While studying in college, she met a man and they fell in love, and following her graduation she exited her 5-year relationship with the client. At this time, she had a university degree, a business, an apartment in the most desirable area of Shanghai, and the first-class urban resident permit. She is now married to the man she fell in love with in college and they live in Shanghai.

For Han, Yu, and many others, sex work was the most expedient means to allow these resource-poor, second-class rural migrant women to accumulate wealth in the shortest period of time, and achieve first-class urban citizenship through conspicuous consumption, acquisition of urban real estate, business ownership, marriage to clients, further education, and ultimately, equality with urbanites.

Case Study Two: Canada

Somebody's got to stand up for these people. They just get walked on… I stand up for what I believe in. (Sherrie)

This section explores the survival strategies our participants employ to manage their complex personal issues and struggles within the web of social, health, and criminal justice services that dominate their lives in many ways. These data demonstrate a series of heart-breaking tensions between what the women want and need and the reality of obtaining these things, which can be hampered by the maze of systems upon which they depend and sometimes resist due to their incongruence with their lived experiences. While some women have gotten into drug treatment, maintain contact with their children, and have safe housing, the precariousness of their lives means that these valuable things oscillate in and out of their lives frequently. This leaves many of them engaged in seemingly endless struggles to regain these and other services, which can reinforce their marginalization and leave them feeling as though "the system" sets them up for failure. As a result, many of the strategies they deploy involve isolating themselves and disengaging from the systems they struggle to access and which do not always make room for them. While some of their decisions can lead to harmful or negative outcomes, their refusal to always or blindly comply with the systems that govern their lives also exemplifies their agency (Wardlow 2006) and resistance to the processes through which they are marginalized.

Trying to Engage: Conformity and Avoidance

Our participants spoke at length about the work involved in accessing, learning about, and maintaining various health, social, and/or criminal justice services, which takes up a staggering amount of their time and daily energies.[1] While their social or case workers often support them as they navigate these complex systems, the women are keenly aware of the inequitable power relations between themselves and their workers. As Vicky astutely said: "They're the ones that are the professionals and that's basically what we need by our side in case they [the government, the courts, their doctors] won't listen to our asses…So basically we have the pull if we have our workers with us." Given that they can yield many benefits while also reminding women of their dependency on others to get what they need, it makes sense that the key strategies the women use to mediate these complex relationships are those of conformity and avoidance.

Conformity

Devising ways to align with service eligibility or requirements was mentioned frequently in our discussions, and this includes tailoring or conforming their behavior and in some cases their appearance to increase the chances of getting services. Kerri's experiences at a hospital where she went to get treatment for an

---

[1] In the course of 1 month, women have between 10 and 30 different appointments to follow up with. Considering the administrative work involved (some of which the women can do, but most forms and paperwork have to be completed by certain providers), transportation issues (costs, poor bus connections, added time on public transport), the range of issues covered in the meetings or appointments (from a food bank voucher to reliving childhood traumas), and the fact that some appointments are prerequisites for others or moving ahead in a different provision stream (and missing one can engender a negative or domino effect on other aspects of life) it is no wonder that women describe being exhausted, frustrated, and often unable to meet the herculean task of keeping some let alone all of their appointments.

abscess capture these issues, along with her frustration with being treated poorly despite her efforts:

> I always thought that by telling the truth, I'd get more respect and that's not the way it works. It's supposed to work if I go in and say, "you know, I screwed up—I had a really crappy day. I did a hit, I missed, and now I'm scared I'm going to lose my arm." I don't go in there swearing or cursing. And I actually go to the point of trying to get dressed up, do my hair and my make-up so I look proper…and it's still, I'm so looked down upon.

Melanie also discussed feeling as though she needed to contain herself in particular ways in the face of stigmatizing treatment from an Ontario Works (OW/welfare) worker, who in many ways controlled her economic future: "I had one caseworker at uh, Ontario Works who…thought I was a liar and if I'm a drug user then I'm clearly just here to scam money-or, you know, awful things like that." When I followed up with a question about how she deals with these situations, she explained:

> I just don't react to it because they're the ones with the money in their hand, right? You can't really um, you can't really say or speak your mind too much because, maybe you're being difficult then they can just, you know [not give her OW]… You don't really talk back to people like that.

Kerri mentioned a different kind of conformity strategy she has deployed to survive in jail, a unique context controlled as much by internal pressure from other inmates as by the guards' coercive disciplinary techniques:

> You would think a guard would want to know if you've got a black eye and a sprained arm, but they'll ask you in front of everybody. So it's like, are you going to be a rat and get beaten again or are you going to say "I fell in the shower?" That's what everybody says: "I fell in the shower", just to keep yourself safe.

Avoidance

The women often discussed avoidance strategies in relation to their struggles with mental health issues, including depression, anxiety, bi-polar disorder, PTSD, loneliness, and suicidality. They described the treadmill they were on with their prescribed medications, which they stopped, started, or avoided taking because either they did not work, they stopped working, the side effects were terrible, or they counteracted the effects of the illicit drugs they were taking. This careful weighing of multiple push–pull factors reflects nuanced decision making and the fluidity of their health-seeking behavior relative to the shifting dynamics of their lives. For instance, Rochelle's decision to avoid her doctor and begin new medications when she was homeless not only makes sense given where she was at, it likely increased her chances of eventual success with the medications. As she explained, "I was homeless at the time and I was worried that it [her new medications] would mess with me, um my mind or whatever…I just now got a place, just starting to settle in now and I can start [the pills]." The complexity of the women's decision-making in this context contests the interpretations of inconsistent intake of medications among street-involved women in many medical and public health studies, which is often reduced to poor decision making skills, lack of access to health information, or "lifestyle" issues (Bungay 2013).

Many women avoided their medications and psychiatric appointments because it is exhausting and hard to keep up with the work that is demanded of them to keep track of and make *all* of the appointments they have. Kerri's retreat from this aspect of systemic engagement was also a way of resisting the authoritative decisions being made for her that she does not agree with: "It just became really hard for me to see Dr. H. on a certain day, Dr. N. on a certain day, and then go to my psychiatry appointment on a certain day. And they were trying to wean me off benzos,[2] which I didn't want to be weaned off, so…I just stopped going." Laura also spoke about standing up for herself with her "mental health doctor…He's all right. I cusses his ass out if he, if I don't like something. I don't do whatever he tells me to do. I'm my own person."

Avoiding the police and legal proceedings was also brought up by several participants. A humorous description of police avoidance came from Jackie, who said "I'm always trying to be nice. Every time there's too many cops around I walk the other way [laughs]!" Kris described a more complicated example of avoiding the law and pressing charges, in this case against a police officer. After learning about the abuse of one of her children she spiraled out of control and was arrested, and then assaulted by an officer on duty. She explains what happened: "He took all my clothes off and made me sit in the cell with no clothes on. I could have charged him, but I'm that kind of person I just say 'oh well, you know, it was my own fault for getting drunk.'" When I asked why she did not press charges Kris said: "If I'd a charged him, Treena, I would have gone to court and then I would have talked about it in front of everybody and me being naked in myself and he left me in there…" That she has to choose between justice and safety, which do not go together within the context of her life, is a powerful reflection on the kinds of "choices" available to socially disadvantaged women like Kris.

Street-Based Strategies

Alongside the strategies of conformity and avoidance used to maneuver through official social, health, and criminal justice systems, our participants depend upon a range of other socioeconomic and sexual relationships, activities, and ways of living in the local street culture. The main strategies employed in this context are sex work and drug use.[3] The degree to which women use these strategies varies across our sample, over time, and within individual women's lives. Some retreat to or become more embedded in street life when they are frustrated with "officialdom," struggle to pay bills, or are battling other issues that are best submerged for a time with intense drug

---

[2] Benzodiazepine, a class of psychoactive drugs sometimes referred to as tranquilizers that includes Valium, Xanax, and Ativan.

[3] The women are engaged in many other interactions and activities; however, sex work and drug use are by far the most prevalent and have the greatest impacts on the women in our study.

use. The relationship between sex work and drugs is complex and when explaining it women most often framed selling sex as the quickest, most lucrative income-generating strategy available to them. As Patty said, "I found that my best way to make the most money." Their earnings were typically used to support or "feed" their addictions (and often those of their boyfriends) and cope with the heavy weight of life. Being high was also identified as a critical prework condition for most women and another motivation for both doing sex work and using drugs.

Drug Use

The use of drugs is a key survival strategy used by our participants. Drugs in this context cannot be neatly separated into categories like "legal" and "illegal" because they overlap on the street and in women's lives. The kinds of drugs our participants use include (1) hard drugs obtained illegally through street networks (i.e., crystal meth, crack, heroin), (2) legal drugs obtained through illicit means (i.e., marijuana, pharmaceuticals), and (3) drugs that are both legal and prescribed to the women (i.e., methadone, mental health medications). The women use different drugs, often in combination with one another, to manage their mental health issues, stave off dope sickness,[4] fit in or socialize, and sometimes escape from life.

When talking about the empty hustle of scoring drugs to avoid being sick, Kerri said: "It hasn't been fun since I was eighteen." Other women appreciate the calm that drugs can bring: "It lets me have peace of mind" (Sherrie) and highlighted their inclusionary, normalizing effects: "It was like the best feeling in the world and I was in love with it…It was the first time I felt normal" (Patty). For Tracey, who no longer does sex work to support her addictions, dealing drugs garners much-needed supplementary income: "The hydro 30s[5] were forty bucks a pill and we cut them in half 'cause no one here would spend forty bucks, but everybody would spend twenty…Unfortunately, you're not helping anyone or whatever but everybody's got to survive."

These accounts complicate dominant public health and societal discourses about the unequivocally negative and maladaptive outcomes associated with all kinds of drugs and all forms of drug use (Degenhardt and Hall 2012; Meyer, Springer & Altice, 2011). It is clearly not as straightforward as this, and these insights into the diversity of women's lived experiences relative to drug use are critical to the development of representative support/treatment programs that reflect their needs.

---

[4] Which can come from being off or not having access to most if not all of the drugs mentioned above.

[5] Hydromorphone, a class of opioid analgesic or pain medications that produce effects similar to morphine (e.g., fentanyl, Dilaudid, OxyContin) and come in pills of varying strength: 30 mg ("Hydro 30s"), 50 mg, and 110 mg.

Sex Work

Doing sex work is one of if not *the* most valuable socioeconomic and sexual survival strategies the women employ. As with other relationships and living situations, their sex work experiences and its place in their life changes over time depending on various systemic and personal factors. Silvia's situation illustrates this well because while she maintained involvement in sex work over the course of many years, the kinds of work she did shifted, in this instance from street-based, drug related interactions to those focused on regular clients: "Well, just addiction, then drug dealers and you know, just opportunity…I've got kids, so the cycles changed and I have someone regular but I don't walk the streets or anything." Vicky's life in sex work is also less directed by her drug-related needs, "You know I don't buy, I'm not running around doing things for drugs, you know to get the money for the drugs anymore. Now it's just if I, you know, feel like doing something then I'll get it." These examples illustrate how integrated sex work is in these women' lives and the ways it transforms, with respect to type and prime motivation alongside other shifting conditions of life.

Poverty and the high earning potentials afforded by sex work were other themes discussed often. Laura plainly stated: "I'm a homeless girl tryna make a livin'", as did Rochelle: "I needed money to get by and for food, and my habit as well, so." Women like Kerrie talked about the tremendous economic pressures on her due to the cost of her drug habit, and that of her partner, along with trying to raise their kids: "For ten years, I supported my ex-husband and myself in the heroin habit, we had three kids and we couldn't be dope sick. So I had to make sure every single day we had at least five hundred dollars." Women were often the breadwinners in their relationships, via sex work, and were used to supporting themselves in desperate situations:

> Got out of jail and he was already hooked up with another girl. Had her pregnant. My house was sold—I signed the papers in jail—I got none of the money. I got no clothes. He literally left me out to dry because he was an asshole. What? You know, so I ended up on the street and I did have sex with men for drugs (Marnie).

The women in our study are keenly aware of the economic value of sex and have used it to their advantage, often when dominant service systems could not or did not meet their needs. As Judy wisely said, "Long story, the money. Money does run the world and vagina does trump all. Like that's just the way it is."

Case Study Three: The United States

US street-involved women actively resist the systematic collusion that restricts their autonomy and citizenship via risks to their health and safety described in Chapter 2. These risks, and women's strategies for dealing with them, are co-constitutive and work in tandem such that each is a response to the other. The women negotiate their restricted citizenship through extrajudicial problem solving and selective enlistment of police aid, working independently, developing a work-related interpersonal tool kit, and accessing healthcare during incarceration or court-mandated addiction treatment. While these negotiations consistently emerge in fieldwork with street-involved women, it is important to mention that these are also a matter of individual personality and the resources that a woman can mobilize for herself, as 26-year-old African-American Jenisa pointed out:

> It does depend on the woman, it just depends on how she feels. Cause some women will just like, bottle it in and just be like, "I'll be okay" and just push it off, push it to the back of their mind, don't let it bother them, and some just let it break'em down...there's really no one to help you.

Extrajudicial Problem-Solving and Selective Enlistment of Police Aid

Denver street-involved women's fear of arrest and general mistrust of the criminal justice system result in selective, restricted enlistment of police aid and primary reliance upon extrajudicial problem-solving measures. Adversarial relations between police officers and street-involved women discourage reporting in all but the most exceptionally violent instances, such as those recounted by 41-year-old Claire, who is White, and 26-year-old Tanya, who is African-American:

> *Claire*: Most women don't. I never did. One time I did, and it was only because a truck driver found me. I grew up in Florida and I was brutally raped by someone that I knew very well. He took me out to the Everglades and I was butt naked, bloody on the side of the highway and a truck driver picked me up. And that was the only reason I reported it.
>
> *Tanya*: I told the police about it afterwards. I told the cop, "I'm out here doin' what I do, but at the same time there's a guy runnin' around here and somebody's gonna end up bein' hurt", and I told him, "I think maybe I got away because I was his first victim."

Both women escaped from men who assaulted them with intent to kill; while Claire's assailant left her for dead on the side of the road, Tanya bit her attacker when he forced her to perform oral sex on him and fled when the resulting pain incapacitated him. Women intergenerationally involved in street sex trading, who consequently often have more nuanced and extensive knowledge about police encounters, sometimes speak about police as allies, within the boundaries of their necessarily adversarial relationship. Twenty-nine-year-old African-American Kyra, for instance, obliquely but significantly referred to how police officers might offer assistance to a street-involved women in need:

> Like you talk about something that you want to make happen, they actually give you good advice possibly, y'know what I'm sayin'? It can't be about criminal things or none of that

because they're cops and if they give that information out, how to beat the case and shit... it won't work.

Women may also call the police in order to exact retribution in extreme cases where a person or group of people has committed an offense against them; as 35-year-old Noelle, who is Native American and African-American, advised:

> If you're all fucked up and beat up, you go to your homeboys. But if ain't nobody gonna have your motherfuckin' back I'll call the motherfuckin' police. I'll take all y'all motherfuckers down. Y'all don't wanna do that, cause people who wanna do somethin' like that, they're doin' something very dirty, and if you're gonna do me dirty, I'm gonna do you fuckin' hella dirty. If I don't have no homeys that have my back, I'm gonna call the motherfuckin' cops, and I'm takin' everybody out!

Rather than enlisting police assistance, women much more commonly engage in extrajudicial problem solving through threatening, or actually committing, violence. Leelee, who is 47 and White, described the need to carry a weapon (ideally an immobilizing and potentially deadly one) in order to avoid rape:

> If I wasn't carryin' a gun or knife or somethin' to protect myself, I would take self-defense classes, so that way I know I can defend myself if I have to. I always wanted to carry a taser, boy. I seen one at the flea market, it was like a pink cellphone and it was this big and it was 500,000 watts. That'll set'em straight! I wanted it but that thing was like $75, but like if it goes to that, it'll pay for itself. Cause I've heard all kindsa stories about girls who get into cars and they get raped, like, I've heard women that've been raped like five thousand times.

African-American Pearlie, who is 52, laughed as she recalled exacting her revenge on a man who had refused to pay her after sex: "I had me a tire iron, and when he came up [to me, later], I knocked the piss outta him!"

Working Independently

Denver street-involved women prefer to work independently and without an intermediary as a means to control their working hours, locations, and income, resulting in a highly competitive environment that limits women's abilities to protect themselves, one another, and share resources. Most women described actual or aspiring intermediaries as offering little in the way of protection or money management opportunities despite their raising women's risks considerably. Neighborhood intermediaries frequently demanded that women earn a set amount of money, referred to as a "quota," which forced women working with intermediaries to stay on the street for longer hours with limited ability to screen clients, increasing their risk of arrest and assault all while giving away their money to an intermediary. Twenty-eight-year-old African-American Dion described the situation of one of her colleagues, who worked with an intermediary in conditions that Dion herself found untenable:

> She would have black eyes and busted lips and I was like [to the intermediary], "why are you sendin' her out there like that?" and it's all because of how much money she brings

back, but sometimes it's hard out there, you don't wanna go to jail. Why would I go to jail just to have a certain amount of money? I can't spend it, cause they'll take it! It'll be pointless. Some days you won't have any money, or maybe $20, and you'll get beat up for that. It's sad…When you have a quota to make, it's either a ass whuppin' or make this money, so they stay out there longer. I would rather just stay out a longer time and just not make money, instead of takin' those kinda risks. I don't wanna take those risks.

Vanessa, who is 28 and White, warned that women working with an intermediary would also face further exploitation due to what she regarded as their inability to conduct themselves as independent and mature adult women:

A woman who knows how to do it on her own can respect herself a little bit better. Because they're making that money and they can be proud of the money that they made. Somebody who's turning around making all that money for somebody that they don't ever get to see [the money] themselves…They got a woman's body but they still act like they're thirteen. And you know who, as a man, is not gonna wanna take advantage of a thirteen year old?

While criminalization actively discourages solidarity among women in ways discussed in Chapter 2, women do create and rely upon social networks. Often these bonds occur in times of crisis, such as following an assault, and revolve around intensified drug and alcohol use, such as 29-year-old Kenya, who is African-American, described:

My homegirl, not too long ago she got raped, but all she wanted to do was get high, take her mind off it, just for somebody to be around her, she was like, "please just don't leave me. Just stay by me." So I just stayed with her all night. That's all she wanted to do was get high, though. Just to numb the pain, just to numb it so you don't think about it. Even though it happened, you don't wanna think about it. But the more dope you do, the more you smoke, the less you feel. Then she finally went home to her mom.

Unfortunately, the high value many women ascribe to working independently creates an environment in which many women blame their peers for complicity in assault, as did 30-year-old African-American Carla:

This dude told her that he had $100 and she didn't want to do anal sex and he raped her, did it anyways. When she came out of there she was screaming, she only had her little shorts on, and I got her into a cab, we went and got another room and it was like, "you have to think of the situation you put yourself in."

Work-Related Interpersonal Tool Kit

Women express well-deserved pride in the intuitive and interpersonal skills they develop in order to protect themselves from violence and arrest and to maximize their access to resources in a heavily policed socio-spatial environment dominated by illegal drug and sexual economies. These skills are themselves products of what criminalization demands of the women, specifically the need to protect themselves in an environment with high levels of violence, much of which stems from the extrajudicial problem solving that regulates the illegal drug economy.

Thirty-one-year-old Corinne, who is White, emphasized the need for women to develop intuitive interpersonal skills:

> I've learned to adapt from good to bad to any walk of life, basically. I can adapt very well and a lot of people don't have that skill. A lot of people are just like, "oh my god, I was taken care of all my life and now I'm here and who's gonna take care of me?", you know? And it's like, "okay, hello!" Reality check! You're livin' on the street, you're a prostitute. Stick up for yourself and defend yourself and learn what it's about instead of pissin' and moanin' about it, because if you keep pissin' and moanin' about it, you're gonna get got over time and time again.

Women frequently used terms like "instinct," "intuition," "radar," or "energy" to describe the process by which they determine how to interact with an unknown client or individual, typically through a combination of environmental factors and luck. Forty-year-old White Raelyn said she avoided going out during the full moon, when "every crazy pulls out of the woodwork," while other women avoided working when it rained, or on particular days of the week. Thirty-year-old Brandy, who is White, described street-based sexual encounters as essentially pragmatic for both provider and client:

> Somebody who is out on the street is knowing what they are fucking looking for, that's it. They're not going and looking on the street for anything else. When they hit the street, they know what they're looking for, and they know what they're willing to pay. If you can meet that criteria, then you got business. If you can't do that, you're out.

Women described the important role of sociality, most notably the ability to casually converse with strangers in ways that put them at ease; as 23-year-old African-American K'Neisha put it, "it's all in how you talk to'em, conversation rules the nation out here." Shirley, who is 43 and African-American, concurred:

> You have to be a good talker, I think, a good talker, because you could change your mind right there and then and say, "I'm gonna go for more money", or whatever. Somethin' like that I'd be afraid of, cause they could try to pressure you and you don't know what might happen next.

As Shirley notes, "what might happen next" remains a constant unknown in many street-involved women's lives, in which the criminal justice system plays an ever-present and undeniably powerful role.

Healthcare during Incarceration or Court-Mandated Addiction Treatment

A significant majority of street-involved women only have sustained access to healthcare and prescribed medications while incarcerated in jail or prison, or during court-mandated drug treatment in transitional housing facilities, which leads some women to describe these criminal justice system encounters as restorative. Twenty-five-year-old African-American Jacqui, who asserted that she "never had a problem with bein' in jail", said:

Case Study Three: The United States

> Jail reserves the age in the body...You could go in jail looking like that but you'll come right out looking like that...you walk in there, being the age eighteen or nineteen, you got five or six years, you gonna come out looking the way you did when you came in...And more healthier... That's what jail does: it rebuilds who you're supposed to be...it's another chance in life to clear your mind and go out there and hope that you're going to be strong and go with what the plan is that God set for you, because everybody find Jesus in jail... and they talk about how they gonna change.

Women do not always succeed in their efforts to seek out healthcare while incarcerated, which for many is one of the few opportunities to do so while they are sober and stably housed. Thirty-seven-year-old White Mindy described her frustration at learning that county budget cuts resulted in her inability to have an HIV test in jail:

> It used to be standard that they gave everybody a HIV/AIDS test, and they don't anymore. And it's very hard to get one. It's to the point where I said I had been brutally raped. This is what I put on the kite [medical request]...I said I had been brutally raped and I had green ooze running down my leg and I still didn't get seen... Would not do it, they said it cost too much these days. And I said, "I just told you, I've been brutally raped." And it didn't matter. I tried my last three times being in jail to get a test for that, just because my boyfriend cheated a lot...I'm not even nervous about tricks- I always use protection, but I'm nervous about him.

Women also attempt to obtain healthcare in court-mandated therapeutic treatment contexts, which often have a transitional housing component. For some women, this involves participation in therapeutic community, which differs from 12-step addiction treatment models by stressing individual responsibility both for decisions made while abusing drugs and alcohol as well as the decision to stop using substances. Therapeutic community features prominently in many US correctional facilities' approaches to addiction treatment, particularly in specialized housing units that solely address these issues, which may rely upon incarcerated persons to manage the treatment and behavior of other incarcerated persons as part of the belief that individuals need to be accountable to one another. This can be problematic due to the power dynamics involved, such that 19-year-old Latina Denise described her experience with a therapeutic community program while incarcerated as "the most traumatic thing that's ever happened to me."

Women who have participated in court-mandated therapeutic community outside the correctional context described humiliating instances of being forced to wear a wall clock on a neck chain for being late, wearing a dunce cap in a corner for failing to convincingly engage with issues thought to cause addiction, being made to clean or stand for hours at a time, or being placed at the center of a circle where other women in the program shout insults. As 32-year-old African-American Ashanti noted, "Shit will break you down to build you back up...it'll fuck you up...don't you think I'm already broke down?" However, she also described how women could successfully complete even the most restrictive court-mandated program, by:

> Runnin' game on'em, y'know what I'm sayin'...It's easy to complete a program. You just tell them what they want to hear...Trust me, you know [what they want to hear], just from like, being around different people. Watchin' different TV shows, y'know what I'm sayin'.

By appearing to participate in their addiction treatment, street-involved women create a feedback loop whereby programs appear successful, even if only because women have learned how to fake adherence to their guidelines.

Discussion

In all three case studies, the women's negotiations of systematic collusion appear to come at significant potential or actual costs to their health, safety, and earnings. In adopting myriad strategies to navigate the many systems and individuals who exert tremendous influence over their lives, women evince competing forces of agency that often introduce new challenges while overcoming or avoiding others. Many of the women's strategies stem directly from the absence or lack of structural supports at the state and local levels and accordingly rely upon social networks embedded in the criminalized socioeconomic context in which they live and work, along with its associated extrajudicial problem-solving measures.

In all three case studies, women's negotiations of systematic collusion rely primarily on the establishment of interpersonal relationships with strategic figures, peers, or clients. These relationships, which can be temporary or lifelong, serve an essential protective function in the absence of social and legal supports available to their peers who are not involved in illicit or criminalized activities. Women may also thrive and achieve socioeconomic independence within or outside of the sex industry as a result of these relationships, as in the Chinese context. North American street-involved women may also experience significant changes to their life circumstances as a result of such relationships, although struggles with addiction, homelessness, and related issues make this less likely.

One significant pattern in all the women's lives involves the formation of protective networks with figures who exercise control over the socio-spatial context in which they sell or trade sex. Hostesses in China frequently forge intimate partnerships with men who enjoy prominent positions in neighborhood gangs and who they can call upon when mistreated by a client or peer. Street-involved women in the United States likewise often work hard to cultivate relationships with purveyors of controlled substances, gang members, or other prominent neighborhood figures as a means to enlist protection and gain status. In the Canadian case study, women alternately engage with social service providers using conformity, when they feel able to meet the conditions of service provision, and avoidance when they cannot. The latter strategy often involves deeper engagement in social networks strongly characterized by sex trading and illicit drug use.

In all of these instances, women employ strategies that involve disengagement from systems that make no room for them, while exemplifying their resilience, resourcefulness, and knowledge. These strategies are also intimately tied to the inequitable conditions associated with criminalization, which not only marginalizes the women but also often leaves them with few options other than to forge alliances with individuals embedded in a criminalized socio-spatial context and who may be exploitative in other ways. As such, the formation of these relationships functions to reproduce the women's criminalized status and exacerbate their already precarious lives.

Women may also forge temporary alliances or cliques with other women involved in transactional sexual activities as a means to engage in mutual aid. In China women form these alliances with relatives or those from their home village, while in North America these center on illicit drug use and sharing of precious scarce resources such as housing. Arrest, incarceration, competition for clients, and the generally divisive environment in which the women live and work tend to make these alliances short-lived despite their indisputable value to the women who participate in them. Insufficient and complex systemic demands likewise often leave women consciously making choices to disengage wherever they can.

Regular clients can also be a source of socioeconomic support to the women although, like the women's other interpersonal strategies, these relationships invite risks as well as benefits. Entering into a relationship with a regular often involves a client's expectation of sex without a condom, increased emotional labor, and other affective performances that resemble an intimate partnership that does not involve the explicit exchange of sex for money. These present a woman with concerns about her health, safety, and what she will do when the contractual relationship ends, in addition to the benefits such a relationship provides in terms of knowledge of a client's preferences, intentions, and the provision of housing or other tangible benefits.

Regular client relationships can be a powerful means by which women in Chinese hostess bars achieve an alternative means of socioeconomic independence, sometimes through substantial gifts of money or other valuable items, marriage, or assistance in obtaining an urban residence permit. North American street-involved women are less likely to achieve this socioeconomic independence because of their struggles with addiction and related problems. Nonetheless, some North American women may engage in less invasive transactional sexual forms as they gain more experience in the more lucrative aspects of sex trading exchanges available to them, such as robbing clients, selling clients illicit substances at a profit, or taking on a managerial sex industry role in which they profit from younger and less-experienced women's sexual labor.

Women in all three case studies negotiate their restricted citizenship and other exclusionary realities imposed by criminalization while attempting to improve their lives in meaningful ways. Yet all too often the systematic collusion that so powerfully shapes their lives results in a situation where making one choice in a particular context means losing other options entirely. These decisions can take place in extremely constrained circumstances that offer little room for autonomy, leaving women with a complex set of conflicting feelings about their lives. The next chapter explores how researchers address these complexities while navigating challenges of their own.

References

Alibayeva, G., C. Todd, M. Khakimov, G. Giyasova, B. Botros, J. Carr, C. Bautista, J. Sanchez, and K. Earhart. 2007. Sexually Transmitted Disease Symptom Management Behaviours Among Female Sex Workers in Tashkent, Uzbekistan. *International Journal of STD & AIDS* 18(5): 324–328.

Bourgois, P., and J. Schonberg. 2009. *Righteous Dopefiend*. Berkeley: University of California Press.

Bruckert, C., and T. Law. 2013. *Beyond Pimps, Procurers and Parasites: Mapping Third Parties in the Incall/Outcall Sex Industry*. Ottawa: Final Report.

Bruckert, C., and C. Parent. 2013. The Work of Sex Work. In *Sex Work: Rethinking the Job, Respecting the Workers*, ed. C. Parent, C. Bruckert, P. Corriveau, M. Nengeh Mensah, and L. Toupin, 57–80. Vancouver: University of British Columbia Press.

Bungay, V. 2013. Health Care Among Street-Involved Women: The Perpetuation of Health Inequity. *Qualitative Health Research* 23(8): 1016–1026.

Cole, J. 2006. Reducing the Damage: Dilemmas of Anti-trafficking Efforts Among Nigerian Prostitutes in Palermo. *Anthropologica* 48(2): 217–228.

Degenhardt, L., and W. Hall. 2012. Extent of Illicit Drug Use and Dependence, and Their Contribution to the Global Burden of Disease. *The Lancet* 379: 55–70.

Dewey, S., and T. St. Germain. 2014. Sex Workers/Sex Offenders: Exclusionary Criminal Justice Practices in New Orleans. *Feminist Criminology* 10(3): 211–234.

Fonner, V., D. Kerrigan, Z. Mnisi, K. Sosthenes, C. Kennedy, and S. Baral. 2014. Social Cohesion, Social Participation, and HIV Related Risk Among Female Sex Workers in Swaziland. *PLoS One* 9(1): 1–10.

Gall, G. 2006. *Sex Worker Union Organizing: An International Study*. Basingstoke: Palgrave MacMillan.

Goldenberg, S., J. Chettiar, A. Simo, J. Silverman, S. Strathdee, J. Montaner, and K. Shannon. 2014. Early Sex Work Initiation Independently Elevates Odds of HIV Infection and Police Arrest Among Adult Sex Workers in a Canadian Setting. *JAIDS: Journal of Acquired Immune Deficiency Syndromes* 65(1): 122–128.

Halli, S., B. Ramesh, J. O'Neil, S. Moses, and J. Blanchard. 2006. The Role of Collectives in STI and HIV/AIDS Prevention Among Female Sex Workers in Karnataka, India. *AIDS Care* 18(7): 739–749.

Holt, T., K. Blevins, and J. Kuhns. 2014. Examining Diffusion and Arrest Avoidance Practices Among Johns. *Crime & Delinquency* 60(2): 261–283.

Izugbara, C. 2007. Constituting the Unsafe: Nigerian Sex Workers' Notions of Unsafe Sexual Conduct. *African Studies Reviews* 50(3): 29–49.

———. 2011. "Hata watufanyeje, kazi itaendelea": Everyday Negotiations of State Regulation Among Female Sex Workers in Nairobi, Kenya. In *Policing Pleasure: Sex Work, Policy, and the State in Global Perspective*, ed. S. Dewey and P. Kelly, 115–129. New York: New York University Press.

Leigh, C. 1997. Inventing Sex Work. In *Whores and Other Feminists*, ed. J. Nagle, 225–231. New York: Routledge.

Lopez-Embury, S., and T. Sanders. 2009. Sex Workers, Labour Rights, and Unionization. In *Prostitution: Sex Work, Policy & Politics*, ed. T. Sanders, M. O'Neill, and J. Pitcher, 94–110. London: Sage.

Majic, S. 2013. *Sex Work Politics: From Protest to Service Provision*. Philadelphia: University of Pennsylvania Press.

Meyer, J., S. Springer, and F. Altice. 2011. Substance Abuse, Violence, and HIV in Women: A Literature Review of the Syndemic. *Journal of Women's Health* 20(7): 991–1006.

O'Doherty, T. 2011a. Victimization in Off-Street Sex Industry Work. *Violence Against Women* 17(7): 944–963.

———. 2011b. Criminalization and Off-Street Sex Work in Canada. *Canadian Journal of Criminology & Criminal Justice* 53(2): 217–228.

Outwater, A., L. Nkya, E. Lyamuya, G. Lwihula, E. Green, J. Hogle, S. Hassig, and G. Dallabetta. 2001. Health Care Seeking Behaviour for Sexually Transmitted Diseases Among Commercial Sex Workers in Morogoro, Tanzania. *Culture, Health & Sexuality* 3(1): 19–33.

Pollini, R., M. Gallardo, S. Hasan, J. Minuto, R. Lozada, A. Vera, M. Zúñiga, and S. Strathdee. 2010. High Prevalence of Abscesses and Self-treatment Among Injection Users in Tijuana, Mexico. *International Journal of Infectious Diseases* 14S: e117–e122.

References

Porras, C., M. Sabidó, P. Fernández-Dávila, V. Fernández, A. Batres, and J. Casabona. 2008. Reproductive Health and Healthcare Among Sex Workers in Escuintla, Guatemala. *Culture, Health & Sexuality* 10(5): 529–538.

Rao Biradavolu, M., S. Burris, A. George, A. Jena, and K. Blankenship. 2009. Can Sex Workers Regulate Police? Learning from an HIV Prevention Project for Sex Workers in Southern India. *Social Science & Medicine* 68(8): 1541–1547.

Roche, B., A. Neaigus, and M. Miller. 2005. Street Smarts and Urban Myths: Women, Sex Work, and the Role of Storytelling in Risk Reduction and Rationalization. *Medical Anthropology Quarterly* 19(2): 149–170.

Sanders, T. 2005. *Sex Work: A Risky Business*. Devon: Willan.

———. 2007. Becoming an Ex-sex Worker: Making Transitions out of a Deviant Career. *Feminist Criminology* 2(1): 74–95.

Tavory, I., and M. Poulin. 2012. Sex Work and the Construction of Intimacies: Meanings and Work Pragmatics in Rural Malawi. *Theory & Society* 41(3): 211–231.

Tucker, J., H. Peng, K. Wang, H. Chang, S. Zhang, L. Yang, and B. Yang. 2011. Female Sex Worker Social Networks and STI/HIV Prevention in South China. *PLoS One* 6(9): 1–6.

Wardlow, H. 2006. *Wayward Women: Sexuality and Agency in a New Guinea Society*. Berkeley: University of California Press.

Weinkauf, K. 2010. "Yeah, He's My Daddy": Linguistic Construction of Fictive Kinships in a Street-level Sex Work Community. *Wagadu: Journal of Transnational Women's & Gender Studies* 8: 14–33.

Williamson, C., and T. Cluse-Tolar. 2002. Pimp-Controlled Prostitution: Still an Integral Part of Street Life. *Violence Against Women* 8(9): 1074–1092.

Youchun, Z., J. Brown, K. Muessig, F. Xianxiang, and H. Wenzhen. 2014. Sexual Health Knowledge and Health Practices of Female Sex Workers in Liuzhou, China, Differ by Size of Venue. *AIDS and Behavior* 18: S162–S170.

Zheng, T. 2009a. *Red lights: The Lives of Sex Workers in Postsocialist China*. Minneapolis: University of Minnesota Press.

———. 2009b. *Ethnographies of Prostitution in Contemporary China: Gender Relations, HIV/AIDS, and Nationalism*. New York: Palgrave Macmillan Press.

———. 2015. *Tongzhi Living: Men Attracted to Men in Postsocialist China*. Minneapolis: University of Minnesota Press.

Chapter 4
Researchers' Negotiations of Systematic Collusion

Ethical Issues in Sex Work Research

The case studies presented in the preceding chapters demonstrate that criminalization and its many effects shape the lives of women in sex work in unique ways depending upon the cultural context in question. Researchers working in locales or countries that criminalize prostitution or other forms of transactional sex also face context-specific realities along with ethical concerns that can be broadly defined as practical, institutional, and political. At the practical level, researchers must juggle relationships with community partners and other gatekeepers while ensuring confidentiality and other protections for participants, which can be difficult given the variant forms of status these groups hold within local research settings.

Researchers may also face institutional barriers at the level of Ethics Review Boards, which exert considerable influence in the receipt of research funding and the ideological framing of sex work itself. Researchers must also confront and navigate the political context in which their work occurs and the uses to which it may be put, along with the challenges it can create among other municipal or state-level players if the findings do not align with prevailing ideologies and funding priorities related to sex work. One of the most important practical ethical concerns researchers must consider involves finding ways to develop bonds of rapport with individuals and the organizations that work with them to carry out the research, which ideally should benefit all participants as well as the researcher.

Many sex industry studies recruit women from fixed site locations, such as an outreach group, shelter, correctional facility, or a third party organization willing to introduce the researcher to women involved in transactional sex (Sanders 2006). Yet such organizations can also deny research requests due to ideological disagreements about sex work, concerns about time commitments associated with conducting research projects, or the potential exploitation of participants (Melrose 2002; van der Meulen 2011). In settings where prostitution is criminalized there may be significant risks for women who speak openly with researchers, including exposure to criminal investigation, arrest or prosecution, and suspicion among their peers if it becomes known that certain kind of information has been shared with outsiders. This is linked with the fact that some women who sell sex are highly sought-after police informants because they may have information about individuals under investigation for drug trafficking, gang-related violence, or other activities the criminal justice system deems more serious than prostitution itself.

Researchers in places where prostitution is heavily policed must make special efforts to protect women's confidentiality due to the possibility that authorities may seize their interview transcripts, field notes, or other data for use as evidence. Long-term participant observation with US street-involved women, for instance, will almost inevitably provide a researcher with detailed information about drug trafficking and other activities of interest to police. US researchers can obtain a Federal Certificate of Confidentiality that protects such research data from a court subpoena or other involuntary disclosure (US Department of Health and Human Services 2014), but, as a New Orleans attorney advised Susan when she mentioned retaining verbatim transcripts that included women's names, "honey, if a prosecutor wants your data, that certificate ain't worth the paper it's written on. Don't make it easy for them- you take those girls' names *out*, unless you're ready to live with sending someone to prison.[1]"

The particular stance regarding sex work adopted by a researcher's institution or potential research funders can prevent the exploration of certain kinds of perspectives and issues, which has serious ethical and political implications. University Ethics Review Boards tasked with reviewing research proposals may reject any inquiry into the sex industry because it is deemed a "problematic area of inquiry" (Sanders 2006, p. 451) or a "high risk" endeavor. These rationales reflect grimly on the issue of academic freedom and institutional support for certain kinds of research, and they can also discredit researchers' reputations by questioning their ability to conduct high quality and ethical research. The particular ideological stance on prostitution or the sex industry more generally adopted by universities or funders can also lead them to explicitly forbid researchers from making evidence-based policy recommendations based on their research. For instance, the Vice President for Research Administration at one of the most highly respected US academic institutions issued a "Policy Opposing Sex Trafficking and Prostitution," which "prohibits the use of any Research Funds to promote or advocate the practice of or legalization of Prostitution" (Emory University 2014).

This policy reflects the US government's refusal to fund research or aid projects that do not take an antiprostitution stance, as part of its official opposition "to prostitution and related activities which are inherently harmful and dehumanizing and contribute to the phenomenon of trafficking in persons" (USAID 2013, p. 47). Researchers interested in transactional sex must carefully consider how to position their work for both

---

[1] Colette Parent and Chris Bruckert faced subpoena of their Montreal sex industry research data when police learned that one of their research assistants had interviewed a suspect in a high-profile murder case about his career in pornography. In the subsequent court case, the Quebec Superior Court argued that research data will only be considered confidential on a case-by-case basis. For more information on this case, see: http://www.cmaj.ca/content/early/2014/02/03/cmaj.109-4717.full.pdf.

their home institution and funders, especially considering that obtaining external funding is often an essential component of securing tenure and promotion at many universities. For US researchers who seek federal funding, this situation is extreme enough to prohibit the use of the term "sex work" because of the government stance that it constitutes "the use of language to justify modern-day slavery, to dignify the perpetrators and the industries who enslave" (US/United States Department of State 2006).

Researchers must carefully consider the implications of their work with respect to whom it represents, the terms on which it engages in this representation, and, once published or otherwise disseminated, the political ends to which their findings may be put. Ethnographic researchers may find that they face particular difficulties in accurately representing the cultural practices of their participants, especially when their lived experiences contradict aspects of the research literature and broader sociopolitical discourse. North American women involved in street-based prostitution and struggling with addiction, for instance, often regard sex trading as a means to an end rather than a defining element of their lives, and often do not self-identify as "sex workers" or even as part of a community of women who sell sex. This mirrors findings from studies with people whose lives are characterized by homelessness, drug addictions, extreme forms of social marginalization, and unresolved mental health issues, but who do not necessarily self-identify as having these conditions or do not want to be defined by them. This presents a challenge for ethnographers who want to accurately portray the insider or "emic" perspective within an analytic context that is informative, ethically sound, and does not reproduce their participants' marginalized status (Bourgois and Schonberg 2007; Fast et al. 2013).

Entering these contested terrains requires that researchers remain mindful of how and where they represent women's necessarily heterogeneous experiences. The sex industry is diverse and even in a singular locale numerous strata exist, differentiated by cost, services provided, demographic characteristics, and risks women perceive to accompany the work (Hoang 2011). Researchers must balance the need to respect women's individual self-identifications by avoiding a false unification or homogenization of their experiences, particularly with respect to working the street, seeking services, or incarceration, given that such research enters a rather crowded field of studies on street-involved women's experiences in public health, epidemiology, or criminology. Such false unification, in which the practices and norms that characterize one form of sexual labor may be extrapolated to other very different forms, risks misrepresenting women's experiences in ways that could have dangerous political consequences.

The way in which particular kinds of research collide with or are subsumed by broader social representations of sex work and the women involved in these complex and highly politicized sets of socioeconomic relationships is another important set of issues to consider. Despite decades of research that demonstrates the inaccuracy associated with dominant portrayals of women in sex work as either fallen victims or vectors of disease, in many sociolegal, health, and cultural contexts they continue to be positioned as vulnerable subjects who must be protected from sexual exploitation (Doezema 2010; Donovan & Barnes-Brus 2011) or as pariahs that threaten the moral order and health of societies (Brock 2009). The gap between research and changing sociocultural ideologies is particularly wide when the issues being examined are contentious and emotive, as with sex work. However, more insidious forces exert a powerful effect on the papering over of certain kinds of research and privileging of others.

This is particularly the case with the neo-abolitionist activists, who have emerged as a well-funded and politically influential global movement in the crusade against human trafficking or "modern-day slavery," both of which are often equated with all forms of sex work (Bernstein 2010; US/United States Department of State 2006). The cooption of sex work with these distinctive forms of exploitation is dangerous because it confuses our understandings of these different phenomenon, contributes to moral panics about sexuality and the movement of different groups of women and girls, and favors sensational debate over evidence-based policy decisions based on in-depth data gathered from researchers, sex workers themselves, and allied advocacy groups (Orchard 2015). The contemporary neo-abolitionist movement is also highly racialized and many troubling parallels have been drawn between it and earlier colonial campaigns organized by White women intent on saving or speaking for a "Third World" Other (Doezema 2001). In a bitter irony, self-identified abolitionists in the United States support criminalization despite the consistency with which it forces African-Americans, as well as other women of color, into the shackles of the criminal justice system for prostitution-related offenses at rates that supersede their White peers relative to population size (US Department of Justice 2012, p. 2).

The case studies that follow document our respective struggles to engage in meaningful long-term work with women who trade sex while working within the often restrictive legal and cultural frameworks that shape both their lives and our own.

Case Study One: China

Sex work researchers are forced to negotiate with systematic collusion both during their research and throughout their academic career. Indeed, many researchers have written about the psychological impacts that sex work research has had on them due to these ongoing negotiations (Bruckert 2002; Dudash 1997; Egan et al. 2006). In this section, I discuss the kinds of negotiations I underwent in order to cope with systematic collusion during my fieldwork and in my academic career. These terrains of negotiations include suspicion, violence, police raids, stigma and marginalization, and encounters with scholars in the academic field.

Negotiating Suspicion

Sex work is not only criminalized, but also politicized in China. During the Republican era (1911–1948), sex work was linked to nationalism, associated with cultural weakness, national shame, and social, political, and even physical sickness (Hershatter 1997; Zheng 2010). During this time, sex work was treated as a social evil that harmed social order, women's rights, and the progress of the Chinese people (ibid.). Communist (1949–1978) and post-socialist China continued to view sex work as a sign of a weak state, holding that it was imperative to demonstrate a strong Chinese state by staging campaigns to eliminate sex work.

In this system of criminalization and politicization of sex work, my research on this subject in China raised many people's suspicion that I was a spy sent by the United States to humiliate China and ruin its global image by exposing its "dark secrets." According to local people, research on sex work carried too much political sensitivity, and they contended that China has endeavored to present a lofty image to the world as a socialist country with a moral system that is superior to that in capitalist countries. Sex work was considered a vice that could only happen in a capitalist country, not a socialist one. Its connections to corruption and government officials' decadence presented a shameful side of the country that the Chinese government wanted to conceal from the world.

I was confronted with two choices: either conducting this research and being called a traitor and a spy, or working on another research topic and being extolled as a patriot. As a researcher, I believe in pursuing truth, not lies, and I see it as my duty to excavate the voices of those oppressed, marginalized, and silenced by an unjust system. I believe my role is to learn from the women, to understand their everyday pain, struggles, and hopes, and to let them speak through my work. Despite local people's well-intended warnings and advice, I embarked on my research, and confronted seemingly insurmountable obstacles from the start. When I traveled to dozens of karaoke bars to talk to their owners, my requests to conduct research in their bars were universally turned down. After these failed attempts, I decided to turn to my friends in the city, hoping they could offer a hand and make introductions for me to the bar owners they knew. However, due to the overall suspicion of me and the political sensitivity of the topic, only one was willing to introduce me to his friend who was a karaoke bar owner. Although I was thrilled, unfortunately, his friend decided to reject my request to conduct research in his bar. These failed endeavors left me frustrated and at the same time worried about the feasibility of this research.

My research topic also made it impossible to interview government officials due to their suspicion of me as a spy. Prior to finalizing plans to conduct research with sex workers, I had made friends with several government officials through several rounds of dinner appointments and gift giving. These officials worked in various apparatuses in the local government. After learning of my research topic, they distanced themselves from me and emphasized that revealing information to me would jeopardize their political positions and political career. Indeed, suspicion of me informed almost all our interactions; once while singing at a karaoke bar with a couple of officials and entrepreneurs, one of the officials suddenly grabbed my purse and began searching inside. I was too taken aback at the time to realize what was going on, and when he did not find anything but a mirror and my keys, he returned my purse. He seemed much more relaxed afterward, and in hindsight I came to realize that he was checking to see if I had hidden a tape or video recorder in my purse.

As time went by, however, I noticed that their suspicion of me diminished and the tension between us mitigated after they experienced my sincerity in dealing with them and my persistence in conducting this research. At this stage, some of the officials openly joked about their previous suspicion of me as a spy; to me, this open, candid conversation marked a remarkable stride from their previously sudden action of investigation and hidden distrust. As time elapsed, they developed trust in me. One political official asked me to tutor his daughter in English, and I agreed. As a return, he, who was a regular customer in karaoke bars and had close relationships with bar proprietors, introduced me to some karaoke bar owners to conduct my research. He also introduced me to his previous mistresses to conduct interviews with them, who were ex-hostesses who now owned businesses. In all these introductory meetings, I fully explained to the owners and hostesses my identity as an anthropologist and my research with sex workers, lest anyone misunderstand the purpose of our meeting.

Negotiating Violence and Police Raids

During my research in hostess bars, I found myself constantly dealing with violence from gangsters, thugs, clients, and police raids. When I worked and lived in Romantic Dreams in the crime-plagued red-light district, hostesses and I were forced to maintain constant vigilance. Most mornings we went to sleep in the hostess dorm upstairs; at times I slept with three hostesses on the sofa in one of the karaoke rooms on the first floor that was rented to clients during operating hours. Before we went to bed, we pushed a couch against the door to prevent gangsters from breaking in. Many times when we heard the sound of gangsters or sudden police raids outside our room, we held our breath and kept the lights shut off. We escaped danger many times, which brought us closer.

One Friday night, as usual, we were sitting in the hallway talking and joking to each other when suddenly waiter Wang burst through the door, yelling: "Everyone upstairs! Fast! The police are coming this way any moment! They are raiding the karaoke bar next door now!" At these words, all the hostesses, including me, frantically raced to our dorm room upstairs and hid under the bunk beds, which served as a hideout in times of police raids. Waiter Wang admonished us not to make any sounds, and we heard him lock the room from outside the door. Everyone was holding their breath, and the room was dead silent. During this time my heart was racing; my mind was twirling, searching for words to respond to police interrogation and expecting police abuse upon arrest. A few minutes later we heard heavy steps coming upstairs. A man asked what was in this room, and waiter Wang answered calmly that it was for storage; after a long silence, their heavy footsteps faded away. No one made any sound for more than 40 minutes, until waiter Wang told us it was safe to come out.

Like other hostesses, I constantly feared attacks by gangsters and clients. On one occasion, gangsters walked into the bar, grabbed my arm, and began dragging me up the stairs toward the sex room, where gangsters raped hostesses and where hostesses provided sexual service to clients. I quickly realized that I was in a crisis situation. Panicked, I did not know what to do but to stare at the bar manager and the bar bouncer to plead for help. Just before the gangsters reached the second floor, they were stopped by the bouncer and manager, who told him that I was their friend, not a hostess. Their intervention extricated me from the impending violence, but the fear lingered on.

Some clients also threatened me during my research. One client selected me to wait on him for the evening, and while we were singing songs in the karaoke room, he asked me to "go out" (a euphemism for providing sexual services) with him. I turned down his request by telling him that I "had a red light signal" (meaning menstruating), a technique and a term that I learned from the hostesses to reject sexual requests. The client was so enraged by my refusal that he threatened me before he left, shouting, "just you wait—I'll be back for you!" His threatening words haunted me for a long time, during which time I elicited hostesses' help to warn me of his presence in the bar so that I could escape in time to avoid his potential assault and violence.

In the end, it was the combined endeavors of bar owners, bouncers, and hostesses who helped protect me from imminent violence from thugs, gangsters, clients, and police raids. Without their help and sacrifices, I would not be able to negotiate through these precarious situations or continue the fieldwork.

Negotiating Stigma and Marginalization

Due to my ethnographic research method of living and working as a hostess in a karaoke bar in the red light district, I found myself stigmatized, marginalized, and shunned as one of the sex workers in the local community, including by my own family members. In the city, knowing that I was enmeshed in the sex industry, my friends started ostracizing me one after another. Some of them distanced me without offering any explanation, while others confronted me directly, telling me that I must be carrying some sexually transmitted infections since I was so close to the sex workers in the red-light district.

When I visited my parents at the end of my research, they shut me in a room and sat me down in front of them, taking turns to lecture me and scold me for turning into a sex worker. They said they noticed a change in me and were severely concerned. They said I was no longer a "respectable" woman who lived on my knowledge, but a sex worker who lived on my face and body. They criticized the kinds of clothes I bought and remarked that only sex workers wore those kinds of clothes. They begged me not to let myself degrade into a sex worker because that was not me. My parents' diatribe, together with my local friends' ostracizing and stigmatizing remarks and attitude toward me, left me distressed and marginalized in the local community. Working as a hostess during my research, I experienced the same kinds of work-related adversities that hostesses encountered, including this hostile and antagonistic environment that hostesses and I were forced to negotiate with on a daily basis.

Negotiating with Scholars in the Academic Field

Over the years in the academic field, I found myself having to negotiate with scholars who hold two kinds of political views on sex work. The first group of scholars holds a romanticized and exoticized view of sex work, whereas the second group holds an abolitionist view. My interactions with these two groups of scholars often times sparked contested disputes and at times sheer hostility from them. In conferences and other academic settings, some scholars from the first group, learning that I conducted sex work research at karaoke bars, often said to me: "Wow! That sounds like so much fun! You must have had a lot of fun and a great time!" Other scholars from this group inquired if I was ever overcome by my sexual desire and engaged in sex work with clients during my fieldwork.

These remarks are indicative of some scholars' political position that glorifies and eroticizes sex work and dismisses the violence embedded in the systematic collusion faced by sex workers. The question about my engagement with sex work seems to offer the scholars not only a voyeuristic pleasure but also an opportunity to further stigmatize and marginalize sex work researchers. To that question, providing a negative answer would run the risk of discrediting sex work, which I believe is legitimate work, and delegitimizing researchers who do choose to engage in sex work during their research. Providing a positive answer would offer an opportunity for others to stigmatize and marginalize me in the academic field. Under such circumstances, I often chose to ignore them or refused to provide an answer.

In the academic field in China and the United States, scholars from the second group often challenged my work by insisting that sex work should be abolished because sex workers are victims in need of rescue. In China, when my initial attempts to conduct research failed, a reputable Chinese university professor offered to help as my gatekeeper and take me into a karaoke bar to conduct research. I was thrilled by this potential collaboration at first, only to find out later when we met to discuss the details that he held a political agenda and expected me to fulfill it. In my meeting with him, he handed me a list of research questions, research goals, and interview questions that were intended to prove that sex work should be abolished as a social evil, and that sex workers should be rescued as victims. After I learned about his political position, I terminated this potential collaboration.

Scholars with this political stance also abound in the United States. At one conference, I was caught in a debate with scholars from this group, who showed pictures and recounted stories of women were trafficked into the sex industry. They argued that sex work should be criminalized in order to combat the trafficking problem and save sex workers, whom they called "sex slaves." In response, I discussed from my own research about how violence stemmed from the criminalization system of sex work, not from sex work itself, how hostesses engaged in sex work out of their own volition, rather than being abducted, trafficked, or forced, and how I believe that sex work is legitimate. My talk did nothing but incite so much anger and hostility from the audience that one of the scholars rose up, pointing a finger at me: "You are the reason why so many under-aged girls are trafficked into sex work!"

Such condemning and denouncing remarks came to be something that I have had to wrestle with in my academic career. I am often sought out by groups in the United States who offer to pay a high honorarium for me to deliver talks about the harms caused by sex work and the victimization of sex workers as trafficked slaves. I do not hesitate to reject these requests, as I find it unethical to betray my research subjects and discredit the legitimacy of their work and the validity of their choices.

Case Study Two: Canada

Many scholars, including those with lived sex work experience, have explored how the divisive and sometimes fanatical forces within contemporary academic and activist sex work circles can negatively impact the health, dignity, and representation of women in sex work (Brock 2009; Ferris 2015; Ray 2013; van der Meulen et al. 2013). The experiences of researchers in this contested, shifting terrain have also been examined, often in relation to the emotional, ethical, and health risks associated with doing this kind of work (Boynton 2002; Dewey and Zheng 2013; Nencel 2005; Phillips et al. 2012; Salmon et al. 2010). Less attention has been paid to the ways in which different groups of people within sex work movements impact how or even *if* we can conduct research in our home communities or local regions, and use our data to generate programmatic and policy-level changes.

This section features two examples from my on-going London research, beginning with my efforts to establish a regional sex work project with a diverse group of community researchers/academics. The second example outlines the frustrating experiences I had when trying to contribute to the development of more representative policies and programming for women in sex work in London. While these experiences are unique in that they happened to me, they also reflect broader ideological and political challenges many of us encounter when doing sex work research. Among the most troubling of these challenges is how women in the sex trade are often excluded from taking part in the research and activist-related processes that have them as their focus. This kind of silencing is problematic for many reasons, namely its reproduction of the exploitative and offensive tendency for people in authority to speak "for" not "with" women and others in the sex trade.

Karma's a Bitch: Negotiating with Regional Radicals

This is a story in several parts about trying to work with a group of researchers/community representatives from the radical-lived experience perspective and the insights I gleaned from this experience. When developing ideas for a grant application a couple of years ago, I contacted researchers and community agencies in three regional cities to see if they wanted to take part in a collaborative project with us in London. Over the course of a year of electronic as well as phone conversations, and an in-person visit to one key community it seemed that they were all on board. However, it became clear that the more radical, lived experience feminists (which is how they self-identified) in one community had ideas about research and community partnerships that were incongruent with myself and others on the team.

They created a charter-type agreement detailing the issues they would support and those they would not, which they insisted all team members sign before they would consider joining our project. This raised red flags among team members because these conditions were being demanded of them and because they reflected an aggressive and non-collaborative approach to relationship building that diverged significantly from how the rest of the team envisioned and have approached community-based research in our respective careers and activism work. Another red flag was raised when I learned that following my visit to their community, during which time I shared with them in confidence some concerns held by many in London about a local volunteer agency set up to support women in sex work,[2] they shared these concerns with those working with the agency. This breach of trust exacerbated the already strained relationship between this agency and others in the service provision community in London. Although we now have good working relations with this organization this situation severely damaged things for a long time, and it also led to the dissolution of our relationship with another community that had been previously on board with the research project. When I organized a teleconference to deal with these issues they indicated that their lived experience superceded any expectations of trust or normative ethical relations and that, basically, they can do what they like. This call and my relationship with these women ended very badly, with them screaming at me for wanting to discuss their decision to divulge this private information while belittling my research.[3]

When I accepted an invitation to give a talk in the city of my foes less than a year later, I had an eerie feeling that one or both of these women would materialize, a foreshadowing of sorts. The title of my talk featured the word "karma," which was intended to capture how "researcher-subject" relationships morph over time as they are made and remade during long-term, on-going research and community engagement. As I looked into the thinly populated lecture room I saw one of them, and she was wearing sunglasses that had a piece of paper taped to them with the word "karma" on it. I did not acknowledge her, which was difficult given her dark presence and unmoving focus on me throughout the 45 minute talk and 15-minute question period. Others were unsettled by her too and upon seeing this woman waiting for me outside the room, the assistant to the organizer of my talk advised us to exit the room via a back door to avoid her. As we hurriedly left the room, looking over our shoulders and talking quickly as we moved through the hallway, I was struck by the strangeness of the scene: two women in their 40s and 50s fleeing from this woman and her predatorial behavior. I also learned that she had been handing out one-page leaflets on campus around the time of my talk, which were designed to look like a recruitment poster but featured slanderous references to my research with women in sex work. She was critiquing the amount of the honorariums I have offered ($20.00), my approach to community-based research, and the overall implication was that I was asking women to divulge their intimate stories in a way that was exploitative (see Fig. 4.1).

---

[2] Primarily about insufficient training and safety-related issues for volunteers and women coming to the drop-in, which we learned about from several women who volunteered at the agency and expressed concern about these issues.

[3] Their condemnation of my work seemed quite bizarre considering their limited success with generating interest among women in their own organization. When I visited them over a year after they opened, they were still brainstorming about how to "get women through the door" and could not answer any of my questions about the dynamics of street-based work in their own city.

Case Study Two: Canada

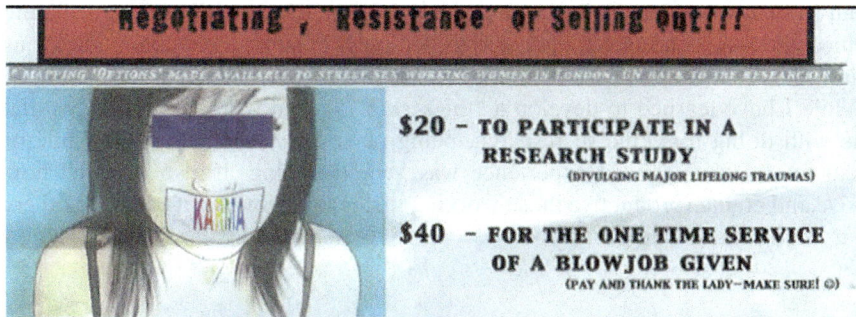

Fig. 4.1 Karmic literature

When thinking about how to respond, I was torn between wanting to "hit back" in some way and knowing that I needed to take the "high road." Upon returning to work I sent a copy of the leaflet to my Director and the Dean of my faculty, provided them with a summary of the events, and we met to discuss an appropriate response. Of the different options suggested, including involving campus police at the host institution (where the woman was a student), we decided to inform her supervisor in writing of the events. Myself and the Dean crafted a letter outlining her threatening behavior and we asked that she be reprimanded or at least spoken to by her program directors and refrain from any communication with me in the future. Her supervisor seemed quite horrified and our requests were adhered to, although in subsequent communications she indicated that the student's version of the story was rather different from mine.

While I have learned to develop a "thick skin" to deal with the challenges that come with doing this kind of research, being personally attacked in the name of radical feminism and lived experience was very troubling. It also revealed how divisive and counterproductive those working inside this movement can be to others also trying to make a difference.

The Sex Work "Plan": Negotiating with City Folks

This story, also in several parts, traces my attempts to contribute to a City plan for women in sex work in London and what I learned about civic politics during this process. My research in London is the first of its kind in the city and I hoped that it would contribute to the development of more culturally relevant and responsive policies and programs for women in the City, who have traditionally been managed under the homelessness portfolio. Several years ago after we completed our first project I organized a meeting with the City employees in charge of the homelessness portfolio and my community partners at My Sister's Place to discuss how we could use our data to generate new programs and policies. Not all women in sex work are homeless and their unique needs and experiences, namely those pertaining to gender, violence, addictions, and the criminalization of sex work, necessitate approaches that reflect their lived realities. I was excited to share our data, which included the women's ideas for improving service structure and delivery (i.e., reducing drug and sex-work related stigma among service providers; streamlining service eligibility criteria; housing outside of the city core; need for more women-only drug treatment facilities). The meeting turned out to be an exercise in the performance of power versus the productive discussion I had hoped for. The City employees spent much of their time educating me about the delicacy of working with vulnerable populations and the near impossibility of selecting committee members for a policy/working group given the contentiousness of the issue of sex work among local service providers.

Although disappointed with the outcome of this meeting I kept in contact with the City folks regarding the creation of a working group, sent them the publications from my research as they were available, reiterated my interest in helping out, and sought their support for my new grant applications. They did not respond to any of these efforts to communicate with them. Two years later I read in the local newspaper that a consultant had been hired to spearhead the development of a plan for sex work-related policies/programming, which was described as a novel initiative by the City to respond to the unmet needs of the women. Somewhat deterred but still committed to being involved, I contacted the City folks again and after several e-mails was given the contact information of the consultant. After spending a considerable amount of time with this woman, who took copious notes about my London project as well as the other sex work research I have done in Canada and India, I was hopeful that I would gain a seat around the working group table. However, when I asked her about this she looked as though I had just asked the most inappropriate question imaginable and we parted ways very uncomfortably. I felt confused by the City's continual dismissal of my offers for help and worried about what they actually had in mind for this seemingly map-less "plan."

These feelings were amplified during the three meetings the City folks held to discuss the "plan," which I attended along with approximately 40 local service providers. Supposedly based upon trauma-informed, women-centered approaches to care, in actuality the plan was a confusing mélange of harm reduction principles and abolitionist ideas designed to help women obtain housing[4] and leave sex work. The fact that no women of lived experience were in attendance was problematic and when this issue was raised we were told that separate meetings were being arranged with them.[5] As we sat at our tables and pored over the large sheets of paper upon which the working principles for the plan were written, we were asked to review their ideas and put our initials beside those we supported—a revealing form of documentation. We were also told that our input mattered, which is why I was taken aback when I asked about Bill C-36 (which passed during the week of the City's first meeting) and was told that the legal framework through which sex work is regulated is not up for discussion in these meetings. The emphasis on the role of the police in the deployment of this "plan" during the meetings added to my confusion and that of others around the table, as evidenced by the many e-mails I received by people in attendance who were shocked about the dismissal of Bill C-36 and had grave concerns about what this plan was about.

Although I attended the rest of the meetings and submitted feedback about the many red flags that continued to arise, the process felt very unsettling and as though there was an ulterior set of objectives driving this "plan." In my distress and curiosity about how others have handled these issues at the City level, I contacted some of my senior colleagues in other Canadian cities. To say they were dismayed by these events would be an understatement, and they were particularly puzzled by the lack of integrated involvement of the women. It has been 10 months since that first meeting and to my knowledge very little has yet to be accomplished and the City did not receive the federal housing funding they were counting on to roll out their "plan."

---

[4] Under the Housing First Policy, developed in the United States and now widely adopted throughout Canada to reduce the systemic hurdles many precariously housed and/or street populations endure before securing good housing (i.e., drug treatment, legal matters, shelter systems, psychiatric assessments). While I am not taking issue with the Housing First approach, it is ironic that the thrust of the new City "plan" picks up right where the old policy left off, with women in the homelessness portfolio.

[5] One such meeting was held on a Sunday afternoon at a seniors' complex located far from the core area where most women live. Despite the inconvenience of this time and place, four women were able to attend.

Good Help Is Hard to Give

The examples shared in this section are not unlike those I have heard from fellow community and academic colleagues, many of whom have also encountered difficult people, agencies, and political forces in their efforts to work with women and others in the sex trade. However, these experiences are not often written about because, I think, they are considered to be part of the job and not something to be complained about. My rationale for sharing these examples is not to complain, but to illustrate how the complex and often counterproductive forces at play in this contested terrain impact the larger social agenda of moving forward and making change related to the well-being, safety, and representation of women in sex work. This uncomfortable truth is worth acknowledging and while we cannot all be on the same page all the time or effortlessly work together, reducing some forms of internal strife could go a long way in generating stronger collective voices and political momentum in this already difficult struggle.

In her account of narco-culture along the Mexico-US border Shaylih Muehlmann discusses how risk is conceived of by the diverse groups of people who are drawn into the drug trade and carry out various "risky" behaviors to support themselves and their families. For some it is built into their inherited socioeconomic status, whereas for others the decision to engage in high-risk practices is more calculated and purposefully deployed (Muehlmann 2014, p. 164). The examples in this section illustrate similar kinds of risks involved with doing sex work research, and how some are the product of local power structures and administrative processes (i.e., city folks), while others are more fluid and deployed in strategic as well as calculated ways (i.e., karma girl). The underlying issues that produce these risks differ, but they were both exercised through insular, exclusionary management techniques that squashed opportunities for meaningful engagement with others involved in sex work research/activism. While many of the risks involved with doing this kind of research and community activism cannot be avoided, being aware of how they operate and what they can look like is hopefully of use to others as they engage in their own ethically minded work with women and different populations involved in the sex trade.

Case Study Three: The United States

Conducting research anywhere in the world with women involved in street-based sex work and struggling with addiction and homelessness presents unique challenges in terms of cultivating mutually respectful relationships, long-lasting bonds of trust, and ensuring that study results contribute to change deemed meaningful by the women themselves. Yet these challenges pale in comparison to the daunting, but not insurmountable, barriers faced by those of us who work in our own communities with women who regularly face arrest, incarceration, and other punitive sanctions as a result of decisions they often make in the context of their poverty, addictions, and precarious housing status.

Criminalization forces researchers to take sides in ways that they may not initially anticipate, and this is particularly true for those who wish to do more than just interview women and publish the results for what, ultimately, constitutes a researcher's own professional gain. Criminalization imprisons researchers within the narrow confines of available resources and the boundaries of the ideals they are willing to sacrifice within a legal regime that pathologizes street-involved women's survival strategies. This is particularly true in the United States, which incarcerates individuals at the highest rate in the world; nearly seven million adults[6] are incarcerated in US correctional facilities (US Department of Justice and Office of Justice Programs 2013).

I did not begin this work with the intention of collaborating with the criminal justice system, and yet as part of my responsibilities at the transitional housing facility I regularly professionally interact with individuals ranging in rank from county probation officers seeking information on women housed at the facility to agents at the Federal Bureau of Investigation who want immediate placement for a victim of sex trafficking. I started this project with a vision of working in activist solidarity with women in full service forms of sex work, somehow imagining that prostitution's illegality could somehow take a backseat to the importance of "the issues." That was easy for me to naively imagine from a privileged position where I did not face arrest on a regular basis as a condition of earning my income. Women working the street also did not self-identify as "sex workers," and instead described their transactional sexual exchanges as the easiest way to earn money to buy drugs for themselves and their associates and to pay for the motel room in which they lived.

Street-involved women had no desire to embrace a collective sex worker identity in order to fight for their rights, as they were already fighting a daily battle to stay out of correctional facilities, remain safe, and preserve their self-respect. Rigid hierarchies along class and ethnoracial lines among women in sex work further derailed my hopes for engaging in participatory work "by sex workers for sex workers." As I spent more time with women on the street, in correctional facilities, and in transitional housing or shelter accommodation, the sex workers' rights movement began to appear both overwhelmingly White and representative of those who worked in venues that provided them with more money, safety, and autonomy than women on the street would ever receive.

This stark difference emerged with unmistakable clarity on a university campus in Denver during an invited panel session I participated in with two women who had extensive experience with indoor and legal forms of sex work. The event revealed some of the complexities involved in insider/outsider privilege, beginning with a faculty member's decision to introduce our panel by magnanimously announcing, to a packed audience, "I consider all three panelists to be my colleagues, not just Professor Dewey," by which I imagine he intended to demonstrate his progressive attitude toward women in sex work—and, of course, did just the opposite.

---

[6] To put this somewhat abstract number into perspective, Hong Kong's population is approximately seven million people.

After this awkward beginning, I decided to remain silent as much as possible in order for the sex worker panelists to speak from their positions of experiential authority. The panelists spoke eloquently about the agential and healing components of their work, and I nodded happily as they talked about their experiences controlling their own income generation activities and sex work careers. An audience member familiar with my research work on the street asked me directly, about halfway through the event, how the experience of the street-involved women differed from the panelists' perspectives. I chose my words carefully, not wanting to contradict the experiences or diminish the power of the other speakers' words, and expressed disappointment that none of the women, who worked just a few miles away from the campus, were able to speak at this venue due to their struggles with addiction and homelessness. One of the panelists interrupted me to abruptly state, "Susan, we have to get away from the notion of the train wreck. Not all sex workers are train wrecks."

To hear the brave and resilient street-involved women I have come to know through my research characterized as "train wrecks" by a woman who purported to advocate for sex workers' rights angered and hurt me. Nonetheless, I felt silenced by my own outsider status as someone who does not make public claims to lived experiences of sex work. These more privileged sex workers on the panel regarded street-involved women as representative of all the worst stereotypes about sex work as violent, demeaning, and rooted in addiction. Accordingly, the panelists wanted nothing to do with the inconvenient realities of the women's lived experiences on the street.

Early in this project I genuinely believed that my conducting long term and intensive ethnographic research with a large number of street-involved women and the professionals with whom they regularly interact would "raise awareness" or "potentially influence public policy," phrases that might appear convincing in a tenure and promotion dossier or at an academic conference but felt increasingly hollow to me because they had little real impact on women's lives. After years of watching police patrol officers arrest women on the street who had nowhere to go and no one to help them access stable housing or other services they needed to self-actualize on their own terms, I decided that interviewing and spending time with the women, publishing what I learned from them, and teaching others was not enough. I wanted action—and this is how I came to work within "the system."

Living in Ideals or Living in the World: Taking Sides

A typical day at my university, which allows me to carry out my pro bono work with the transitional housing facility, involves the usual responsibilities of teaching classes, attending meetings, and supervising students. It almost always also involves returning calls to women working the streets or escorting, or to professionals from a District Attorney's office, the Federal Bureau of Investigation, or a Sheriff's Department in another city, all to advocates seeking a safe and long-term place for women. Some of these women are testifying in criminal cases against an intimate partner. Caught in the vortex of state or federal cases, many of the women these professionals refer to me are understandably distraught when we speak on the phone.

In one striking instance, a woman explained her extreme ambivalence regarding a prosecutor's decision to seek the death penalty for the man who almost beat her to death when she did not bring home several thousand dollars one night—his execution would mean leaving her child fatherless. As the wheels of a state or federal court case creak into motion in the women's lives, often through no choice of their own, the "ain't no man about to run me around" street ethos that I so admire quickly evaporates. The women I regularly speak to who are enmeshed in criminal cases clearly recognize that the criminal justice system's power far exceeds any resources they could potentially mobilize.

I was both honored and conflicted when, in summer 2014, the transitional housing facility's director asked me if I would consider filling the intake coordinator position, which effectively made me the sustained point of contact for all women interested in entering the program. It was a dream come true: a chance to help women make the kinds of real and meaningful changes to their lives that they had talked to me about in interviews and other research contexts. My socialization process at the facility over the years allowed me to clearly understand that facility staff had no choice but to work with the criminal justice system that governs the women's lives. I knew that the facility could not exist if it did not engage in mandatory random drug testing, reporting to probation, and enlist the support of faith-based groups, which in the United States provide a considerable number of social services due to limited state support for those struggling with homelessness and addiction. Yet I only realized this after several years of thinking that these practices constituted abusive demonstrations of power and control. It was only after listening to some of the women tell me that they considered their encounters with social service providers, and even the criminal justice system, important aspects of addiction recovery that I began to change my view, especially as I realized that no self-identified feminist or sex worker-run programs provided housing and other basic services to street-involved women.

Taking on the unpaid position required that I become an assertive decision maker and strong advocate, constituting a sharp departure from the conflict avoidant personality that I thought had served me well as an academic. My research had already familiarized me with the cultural norms and rules of engagement on the street, but to succeed as the intake coordinator I also needed to master work-related norms among criminal justice professionals and social service providers. In practice, this means navigating the regularity with which probation officers and public defenders dismissively tell me that a client will remain incarcerated until the facility had space available for her. I was initially shocked that sometimes this could mean an additional six months of incarceration and begrudgingly accepted that most criminal justice professionals felt it was my, rather than their, responsibility to find alternative accommodation for a woman in the free world. I also advocate for women in their interpersonal relationships; when a woman still working the street calls from an intimate partner's cell phone and asks that I speak with him, I never hesitate. I know that the complexities of such relationships, which sometimes involve the woman turning over all her earnings to her intimate partner, means that she might not seek services again if he does not allow her to do so.

Working effectively as a social service provider meant that I needed to learn how to carefully maintain interpersonal boundaries with the women and their loved ones, often in direct opposition to my research encounters. During my research with the women I never hesitated to show emotion or share personal information about my own life experiences, which enhanced rapport between us. In my intake coordinator role, emotional reactions (particularly tears) or self-disclosure with women seeking services while on the street or incarcerated has the potential to legitimately undermine women's confidence in my abilities to provide them with assistance. Engaging in this professional transition from a conventional ethnographic researcher to a frontline social service provider created a new set of ethical and career-related concerns, which initially raised some difficult questions. Would my colleagues at the university regard my time commitment to my intake coordinator position as unconnected to real scholarship, or even as a charitable hobby that had nothing to do with my research? What would my sex work research colleagues say about my involvement with a faith-based facility that worked with the criminal justice system? Fortunately, I enjoy supportive colleagues and a collegial work environment that prioritizes meaningful social engagement, and most sex work research colleagues seem to understand the considerable restrictions placed on doing this kind of work in the United States.

Yet these questions reemerged powerfully during a talk the facility's Executive Director gave at a university campus, when I watched as she faced criticism from academics and students who had no experience working with the issues that street-involved women face. As I listened to the audience criticize mandatory drug testing and prohibitions on women engaging in sex work while in the program, I was viscerally struck by the privileges academics enjoy in making such critiques without offering any realistic alternatives. I firmly support academic freedom and the right to engage in critique, but the more time I spent with street-involved women who express a deeply felt need to get some help, any help, on their terms, the more frustrating such critiques appear when accompanied absence of action.

Taken together, these experiences taught me that researchers have a choice to make between living in an imperfect world characterized by counterproductive policies and living in the confines of ideals often insipidly characterized as "social justice." These ideals, while noble, carry little weight in the lives of those most impacted by the criminal justice system and the havoc it wreaks. To the brave and resilient street-involved women I have come to know over the years, what matters most is a safe place to sleep, something to eat, and hopefully a chance at a better life. I have found that those who most vociferously critique the structures that systematically deny women these basic needs fail to remember that someone must meet them, all while working in the confines of a criminalized legal regime.

"Expert Testimony"

One of the most sought-after academic privileges involves ascending to expert status, whereby journalists and other professionals seek insights into an issue based upon a researcher's published conclusions. Several years prior to receiving tenure, I was delighted when an attorney requested that I testify as an expert witness in a trafficking case prosecuted at the state (rather than federal) level; this, I thought, was evidence that I had finally "arrived" as a sex work researcher. This initial enthusiasm quickly transformed into tangled morass of ethical concerns as I carefully read her client's indictment and transcripts of grand jury testimony, which included accounts from high-ranking police officers who I had long wanted to interview as part of my then-ongoing research. The attorney offered me a substantial hourly rate in exchange for my agreement to testify that her client, accused of sex trafficking underage girls who were just a few years younger than him, had acted in ways sanctioned by cultural norms that prevail in the context where he had facilitated the young women's sex trading activities.

This case presented me with a serious and multilayered ethical dilemma, as testifying on behalf of a man accused of trafficking minor girls would have professional consequences by potentially harming my reputation in the field of Gender & Women's Studies and alienating the criminal justice professionals I regard as an essential part of my research. In the clear-cut world of the courtroom, which makes no allowances for the standard academic characterization of "it's complicated," the fact that the girls in question were under 18 (although the accused was not much older) would likely combine with prosecutorial enthusiasm to ensure a conviction given the amount of evidence police had gathered. I knew all of this as I read the documents the attorney shared with me and finally opted out when a friend who had practiced law rhetorically asked me what I knew was the fundamental question that would arise for others regarding the case: "Susan, do you want to defend men who traffic underage girls?"

A few years later, I enjoyed a friendly rapport with one of the senior vice detectives who had built the case in which I had opted not to testify. We were leaving a campus classroom where we had just spent 3 hours engaging with students in a class I teach on sex work when I asked him if he would have interacted with me had I chosen to testify. "No," he said, with surprising firmness and sounding remarkably like my career police officer father, "but I know that you know better than to defend bad guys." Ideological positions not of our own making determined the parameters of our relationship in ways that mirror both the criminal case itself and the social services available to women entangled in the criminal justice system.

These ideological parameters so vigorously and deeply divide researchers who work with women in the sex industry that nearly every academic publication includes a requisite paragraph or two that describes the author's position on various "sides" typically taken in these debates, such as abolitionism, sex workers' rights, and harm reduction. All researchers experience feelings of frustration and possibly even ineffectiveness upon receiving a manuscript or grant proposal rejection and I hesitate to write about my own experiences with this lest I appear embittered by my experiences, or, worse still, entitled. Simply put, at this point in my career I, like many other researchers who oppose the abolitionist stance, know that certain feminist journals are off-limits if I want to publish work that features the complexities of street-involved women's lives due to the gatekeeping that abolitionist peer reviewers undertake. Hence the fight continues, on multiple battlegrounds.

Discussion and Concluding Thoughts

One of the most compelling things that the case studies presented here illustrate is the complex and intertwined personal, social, and political forces that coalesce in and through research with women who sell or trade sex. In this chapter we have relayed the difficult sets of experiences regularly accompanying our fieldwork which, in many instances, goes far beyond the normative and emotional bounds of what many academics consider "research." Our work continues to require all of us to make tremendous personal, emotional, ethical, and political sacrifices while we remain deeply engaged in the lives of women who face struggles far greater than our own.

Each of the case studies underscores the multiple barriers and personal challenges we face while attempting to offer full ethnographic portrayals of women's nuanced life worlds. Tiantian Zheng has experienced research colleagues' exoticization of her research in conjunction with accusations of being a US spy and an embarrassment to her family and friends in China. Treena Orchard continues to feel at risk for numerous forms of harassment from neo-abolitionists and other politically charged groups who disagree with her approach to community-based research. Susan Dewey morally grapples with working in a position that requires her to implement the US criminal justice system's prevailing punitive-therapeutic approach while providing services at a transitional housing facility. While each example is unique to its cultural context, remarkable consistency exists with respect to our experiences working in a volatile and highly charged field.

We have all faced practical, institutional, and political negotiations that played instrumental roles in shaping the research findings and accounts presented here. In a number of instances, our research proceeded in unexpected forms and with resistance from unanticipated sources. Both Zheng and Dewey faced the ever-present threat of violence in their participant observation, where their gender and age fit the profile of many women who sell or trade sex, and all three researchers experienced "guilt by association" in their stigmatization as women associated with the sex industry.

As with many other sex industry studies, we built bonds of rapport with women after receiving permission to meet with them through a gatekeeper. Zheng was surprised when the most effective gatekeeper in her study proved to be the hostesses' clients rather than the hostesses themselves. For many good reasons detailed in preceding chapters, women who sell or trade sex may mistrust researchers, and yet she had not expected that hostess bar workers would reject her when she attempted to form relationships with them. Her persistence, combined with introductions from the hostesses' clients, finally ensured that she could conduct participant observation while living and working in three hostess bars.

In the United States and Canadian case studies social service providers filled this gatekeeper role, followed by the establishment of long-term research relationships and friendships with many women Orchard and Dewey initially interviewed. Both researchers initially struggled with the absence of sex workers' rights groups willing to collaborate with them in sustained and meaningful ways. Dewey in particular felt extremely conflicted about working with a faith-based transitional housing facility that serves as many of its street-involved residents' only alternative to incarceration, before slowly coming to the realization that self-identified feminist and sex workers' rights groups offered no options for women who needed housing, addictions or other therapeutic treatment, or basic medical care.

Institutional and political negotiations continue to inform all of our respective projects. In the Chinese case study, Zheng had to make the difficult choice between accurately representing the women's lived experience or adhering to state-sanctioned abolitionist views of the sex industry as inherently exploitative and abusive to women. This tension characterizes all three case studies. In the US case study, Dewey had to come to terms with the virtual impossibility of receiving federal funding to conduct research with street-involved women that did not further pathologize them by focusing on issues related to their health risks or criminal justice system encounters. In the Canadian case study, Orchard experienced similar restrictions in her efforts to form partnerships with other agencies as a result of the trafficking paradigm's dominance.

There are numerous reasons for the challenges that we faced as researchers, yet these experiences singularly draw attention to very wide gaps between and within the different factions engaged in sex work research, activism, and service provision. The examples presented here do not cast much encouraging light on the situation, given that the field is characterized by as much unproductive fighting and systemic injustice as it is by high quality research that captures the diversity of women's experiences in the sex trade. There are lessons here though, and our work that details how we have maneuvered within these contested terrains helps to reveal the lived experience of researchers within the exclusionary regime and how, like the women with whom we work, we are also caught up in powerful systems of collusion.

Taken together, our three case studies presented in tandem with evidence collected by researchers from throughout the world clearly demonstrate that the conditions of criminalization force women who sell or trade sex into unacceptably dangerous, dehumanizing, and stigmatizing conditions through morality-based legislation that offers no discernible benefits to any society in which it has been implemented.

References

Bernstein, E. 2010. Militarized Humanitarianism Meets Carceral Feminism: The Politics of Sex, Rights, and Freedom in Contemporary Antitrafficking Campaigns. *Signs* 36(1): 45–71.

Bourgois, P., and J. Schonberg. 2007. Intimate Apartheid: Ethnic Dimensions of Habitus Among Homeless Heroin Injectors. *Ethnography* 8(1): 7–31.

Boynton, P. 2002. Life on the Streets: The Experiences of Community Researchers in a Study of Prostitution. *Journal of Community & Applied Social Psychology* 12: 1–12.

Brock, D. 2009. *Making Work, Making Trouble: Prostitution as a Social Problem*, 2nd ed. Toronto: University of Toronto Press.

Bruckert, C. 2002. *Taking It off, putting It on: Women in the Strip Trade*. London: The Women's Press.

Dewey, S., and T. Zheng. 2013. *Ethical Research with Sex Workers: Anthropological Approaches*. New York: Springer.

Doezema, J. 2001. Ouch! Western Feminists' 'Wounded Attachment' to the 'Third World Prostitute'. *Feminist Review* 67: 16–38.

_____. 2010. *Sex Slaves and Discourse Masters: The Construction of Trafficking*. London: Zed Books.

Donovan, B., and Barnes-Brus, T. 2011. Narratives of Sexual Consent and Coercion: Forced Prostitution in Progressive-Era New York City. *Law & Social Inquiry* 36(3): 597–619.

Dudash, T. 1997. Peepshow Feminism. In *Whores and Other Feminists*, ed. J. Nagle, 98–118. New York: Routledge.

Egan, D., K. Frank, and M. Johnson (eds.). 2006. *Flesh for Fantasy: Producing and Consuming Exotic Dance*. New York: Thunder's Mouth Press.

Emory University. 2014. *Policy 7.16-Policy Opposing Sex Trafficking and Prostitution*. https://policies.emory.edu/7.16.

Fast, D., J. Shoveller, W. Small, and T. Kerr. 2013. Did Somebody Say Community? Young People's Critiques of Conventional Community Narratives in the Context of a Local Drug Scene. *Human Organization* 72(2): 98–110.

Ferris, S. 2015. *Street Sex Work and Canadian Cities: Resisting a Dangerous Order*. Edmonton: University of Alberta Press.

Hershatter, G. 1997. *Dangerous Pleasures: Prostitution and Modernity in Twentieth-Century Shanghai*. Berkeley: University of California Press.

Hoang, K. 2011. "She's Not a Low-Class Dirty Girl!": Sex Work in Ho Chi Minh City, Vietnam. *Journal of Contemporary Ethnology* 40(4): 367–396.

Melrose, M. 2002. Labor Pains: Some Considerations on the Difficulties of Researching Juvenile Prostitution. *International Journal of Social Research Methodology* 5(4): 333–351.

Muehlmann, S. 2014. *When I Wear My Alligator Boots: Narco-Culture in the US-Mexico Borderlands*. Berkeley: University of California Press.

Nencel, L. 2005. Feeling Gender Speak: Intersubjectivity and Fieldwork Practice with Women Who Prostitute in Lima, Peru. *European Journal of Women's Studies* 12(3): 345–361.

Orchard, T. 2015. The Role of "Children" in Global Sex Work and Trafficking Discourses. *Open Democracy-Beyond Trafficking and Slavery*. https://opendemocracy.net/beyondslavery/treena-orchard/children-in-global-sex-work-and-trafficking-discourses.

Phillips, R., C. Benoit, H. Hallgrimsdottir, and K. Vallance. 2012. Courtesy Stigma: A Hidden Health Concern Among Front-Line Service Providers to Sex Workers. *Sociology of Health & Illness* 34(5): 681–696.

Ray, A. 2013. *Prose & Lore: Memoir Stories About Sex Work*. New York: Red Umbrella Project.

Salmon, A., A. Browne, and A. Pederson. 2010. "Now We Call It Research": Participatory Health Research Involving Marginalized Women Who Use Drugs. *Nursing Inquiry* 17(4): 336–345.

Sanders, T. 2006. Sexing Up the Subject; Methodological Nuances in Researching the Female Sex Industry. *Sexualities* 9(4): 449–468.

US Department of Health & Human Services. 2014. *Certificates of Confidentiality: Frequently Asked Questions*. http://www.hrsa.gov/publichealth/clinical/HumanSubjects/faqs.html.

US Department of Justice. 2012. *Arrest in the United States, 1990-2010*. http://www.bjs.gov/content/pub/pdf/aus9010.pdf.

US Department of Justice, Office of Justice Programs. 2013. Correctional Populations in the United States, 2012. http://www.bjs.gov/content/pub/pdf/cpus12.pdf.

US/United States Department of State. 2006. *A Statement on Human Trafficking-Related Language*. http://2001-2009.state.gov/g/tip/rls/rm/78383.htm.

USAID (United States Agency for International Development). 2013. *Standard Provisions for US Nongovernmental Organizations*. http://www.usaid.gov/sites/default/files/documents/1864/303maa.pdf.

van der Meulen, E. 2011. Action Research with Sex Workers: Dismantling Barriers, Building Bridges. *Action Research* 9: 370–384.

van der Meulen, E., E. Durisin, and V. Love (eds.). 2013. *Selling Sex: Experience, Advocacy, and Research on Sex Work in Canada*. Vancouver: University of British Columbia Press.

Zheng, T. 2010. Knowledge, Culture, and Change: State Management of the Entertainment Industry in China's Past and Present. *The International Journal of Knowledge, Culture, and Change Management* 10(1): 495–512.

Index

A
Acquired immune deficiency syndrome (AIDS)
  injection drug, 13
  laws, 34
  medial/health-related fields, 16

B
Bedford V Canada, 14
Bill C-36 Protection of Communities and Exploited Persons Act, 14

C
Canadian sex workers
  health and safety
    drug user identity, 36
    health care providers, 36
    laws and safety, 38–39
    MMTs, 37–38
    personal safety issues, 38
    police, interactions with, 39–40
  negotiating systematic collusion
    avoidance, 61–62
    conformity, 60–61
    criminal justice services, 60
    drug use, 62–63
    doing sex work, 63–64
    street-based strategies, 62
    survival strategies, 59
  researchers' negotiations
    City plan, 86–87
    counter productive forces, 88
    regional radicals, 83–86

Chinese sex workers
  condom use, 53
  health and safety
    exploitative environment, 32–33
    group disaffiliation, 33
    health risks, 34–35
    violent working environment, 30–32
  negotiating systematic collusion
    contractual relationships with regular clients, 57
    protection networks, 54–55
    temporary alliances, 55–57
    urban citizenship, 58–59
  researchers' negotiations
    scholars in academic field, 81–82
    stigma and marginalization, 81
    suspicion, 78–80
    violence and police raids, 80–81
Colfax Avenue, 19
Condom-less sex, 52
Contractual relationships, 57
Criminalization forces researchers, 89
Crossing Colfax, 19

D
Dalian, 7
Denver After Dark, 19
Diversion court, 21

E
East of Adelaide, 13
Ethnographic context
  dalian, 7

Ethnographic context (*cont.*)
  Denver, Colorado, 17
  East Colfax Avenue, 18
  East of Adelaide, 13
  karaoke bar entertainment industry, 8
  London, 12
  police and regulation, sex trade, 20
  policing and regulating sex work, 9
  regulation, of sex work, 14

F
Feminist anthropologists conducting research, 6

G
Golden road, 19

H
Health and safety
  Canada
    drug user identity, 36
    health care providers, 36
    laws and safety, 38–39
    MMTs, 37–38
    personal safety issues, 38
    police, interactions with, 39–40
  China
    exploitative environment, 32–33
    group disaffiliation, 33
    health risks, 34–35
    violent working environment, 30–32
  harm reduction, 27
  legal status on, 27–29
  police confiscation of condoms, 29
  screening clients, 29
  Sonagachi Project, 28
  Soros Foundation-funded participatory project, 28
  United States
    disrupted peer solidarity, 42–43
    HIV status, 45
    information sharing, 43–45
    police aid and reporting, 41–42

I
Indian sex workers, 53

K
Karaoke bar entertainment industry, 8

M
Methadone maintenance programs (MMTs), 37–38

N
Negotiating systematic collusion
  avoiding police arrest, 51
  bottom bitch status, 54
  Canada
    avoidance, 61–62
    conformity, 60–61
    criminal justice services, 60
    drug use, 62–63
    doing sex work, 63–64
    street-based strategies, 62
    survival strategies, 59
  China
    contractual relationships with regular clients, 57
    protection networks, 54–55
    temporary alliances, 55–57
    urban citizenship, 58–59
  outdoor and indoor sex venues, 52
  regular clients, 52
  rights movement, 53
  self-care, forms of, 53
  Tanzanian sex workers, 53
  United States
    court-mandated addiction treatment, 68–69
    extrajudicial problem-solving, 65–66
    healthcare during incarceration, 68–69
    work independently, 66–67
    work-related interpersonal tool kit, 67–68
  Uzbekistan, 53
Network of Sex Work Projects, 54
Nigerian sex workers, 52
Nordic Model, 2

P
Police arrest, 51
Police raids, violence and, 80–81
Prostitution, 2
Public Security Bureau, 10

R
Researchers' negotiations
  Canada
    City plan, 86–87

Index

counter productive forces, 88
regional radicals, 83–86
China
  scholars in academic field, 81–82
  stigma and marginalization, 81
  suspicion, 78–80
  violence and police raids, 80–81
ethical issues, 75–78
United States
  criminalization forces researchers, 89
  expert testimony, 92–93
  living in ideals, 90–92
  street-involved women, 89
Rights movement of sex workers, 53
Romantic dream, 9

S

Sanpei xiaojie, 8
Sex work
  criminalizing prostitution impacts, 3
    avoid arrest, 3
    offenses, 4
    police scrutiny, 4
    stigma attitudes, 4
  ethnographic context
    dalian, 7
    Denver, Colorado, 17
    East Colfax Avenue, 18
    East of Adelaide, 13
    karaoke bar entertainment industry, 8
    London, 12
    police and regulation, sex trade, 20
    policy and regulation, 9
  legal and public policy responses
    anti-prostitution legislation, 3
    criminalization, 2
    decriminalization, 2
    legislative and regulatory mechanisms, 1
    prostitution, 2
  methodology
    capturing field, 16
    interviews with women, 15
    service provider interviews, 16
    socio-demographic profile, of women, 15
  police and regulation, 9, 14
  systematic collusion, within exclusionary regimes, 5
Swedish model, 2

T

Tanzanian sex workers, 53

U

United States sex workers
  health and safety
    disrupted peer solidarity, 42–43
    HIV status, 45
    information sharing, 43–45
    police aid and reporting, 41–42
  negotiating systematic collusion
    court-mandated addiction treatment, 68–69
    extrajudicial problem-solving, 65–66
    healthcare during incarceration, 68–69
    work independently, 66–67
    work-related interpersonal tool kit, 67–68
  researchers' negotiations
    expert testimony, 92–93
    living in ideals, 90–92

V

Violence, 80–81

CPSIA information can be obtained
at www.ICGtesting.com
Printed in the USA
LVOW02s2332140116
470742LV00014B/502/P